D0590744

MADHUR JAFFREY
INDIAN RECIPES

BOOKS FOR REAL COOKS

PAVILION

Pavilion Books for Real Cooks

Published in Great Britain in 1994 by
PAVILION BOOKS LIMITED
26 Upper Ground, London SE1 9PD

Text © Madhur Jaffrey 1994

Recipes originally published by Pavilion in
A Taste of India

Design by Write Image
Jacket photograph © Gus Filgate

All rights reserved. No part of this publication may
be reproduced, stored in a retrieval system, or
transmitted, in any form or by any means, electronic,
mechanical, photocopying, recording or otherwise,
without the prior permission of the copyright
holders.

A CIP catalogue record for this book is available from
the British Library

ISBN 1 85793 3974

Printed and bound by WBC Printers, UK

2 4 6 8 10 9 7 5 3 1

This book may be ordered by post direct from the
publisher. Please contact the Marketing Department.
But try your bookshop first.

CONTENTS

FOREWORD

From childhood, an Indian is exposed to more combinations of flavours and seasonings than perhaps anyone else in the world. Our cuisine is based on this variety, which, in flavours, encompasses hot-and-sour, hot-and-nutty, sweet-and-hot, bitter-and-sour and sweet-and-salty. The Indian genius lies not only in squeezing several flavours out of the same spice by roasting it, grinding it or popping it whole into hot oil, but in combining seasonings – curry leaves with popped mustard seeds, ground roasted cumin seeds with mint, ginger and garlic with green chillies – to create a vast spectrum of tastes. It is this total mastery over seasonings that makes Indian foods quite unique.

If the choice of seasonings gives one kind of variety to Indian foods, regional traditions give it quite another. The country is vast, with each state like each European nation, having not only its own language, culture and foods, but its own history, its own unique geography and its own set of dominant religions. Although the whole country has in common the total command over spices and seasonings, cooking styles can vary radically from state to state. In the temperate state of Kashmir, tucked into the highest mountains in the world, I have eaten a wonderful dish of dried turnip rings cooked with sun-dried tomatoes. In tropical Tamil Nadu in the South, where the needs of the body are quite the opposite, I have dined on superb crabs poached in a tart tamarind broth. Even within states, some foods are common to most of the people while others are cooked only by special communities.

It is a pity that most Indian restaurants scattered across the world do not reflect this rich variety. While Indian restaurant food can be quite good, it is a world unto itself. India hides its real food – and the best food – in millions of private homes, rich and poor, scattered across its provinces, and it is this kind of food I have selected for this book.

All Indian food is served with either rice or bread or both, following each other in succession. In the North, it is wholewheat breads, such as *chapatis* and *parathas*, that are commonly eaten, and in the South, it is plain rice. The traditional Indian bread used to be flat, baked on cast-iron griddles rather like tortillas. The Muslims introduced ovens where sour dough and plain breads – such as *naans* and *shirmals* – could be baked. The Europeans outdid the Muslims, coming in with fat, yeasty loaves, called *dubble roti*, 'double bread', by the Indians and used to mop up the juices of many spicy stews. I remember that one of our favourite treats as children was to come home from school, kick off our restricting shoes and socks and pad in our loose Indian sandals to the pantry, where on obliging oven kept the leftovers for our after-school snacks. Sometimes there were *chapatis*, into which we would roll up some *sookhe aloo*, dry, well-spiced potatoes, and then gobble them up. At other times, we would slice off the end of a crusty *dubble roti*, hollow it out and fill it with meat korma topped with mango pickle.

At most Indian meals, aside from the meat, vegetables, split peas and rice or bread that are served, there are invariably relishes, yoghurt dishes, pickles and chutneys. They round off the full cycle of flavours and textures, adding bite, pungency and often vital vitamins and minerals as well. We eat with our hands – with the right hand, specifically, the left being used to pick up glasses of water or to serve ourselves more food.

In these recipes, I have tried to show the great

range of cooking in the vast Indian subcontinent, as well as the intricate balance of flavours and textures in individual dishes. I know Indian foods from all the different regions will thrill your palates – they may well uplift your soul.

Madhur Jaffrey
London,
November 1993

SOUPS AND STARTERS

Sarki

COLD SUMMER SOUP WITH CUCUMBERS AND TOMATO

SERVES 5–6

13 oz/ 2 cups/
375 g skinned *toovar
dal* or yellow split peas,
picked over, washed
and drained

½ tsp/ 2.5 ml ground
turmeric

½ tsp/ 2.5 ml ground
roasted cumin seeds

2 tbs/ 30 ml lemon juice
or a bit more, as desired

1 ¼–1 ½ tsp/ about
6–7 ml salt

freshly ground black
pepper

1 fresh hot green chilli,
very finely chopped

2 spring onions
(scallions)

8 oz/ 225 g, 1 large
tomato

2 small pickling
cucumbers or 7 oz/
200 g cucumber with not
very mature seeds

2 tbs/ 30 ml chopped
fresh green coriander
(Chinese parsley)

about 6 tbs/ 90 ml plain
yoghurt

The Bohris, Muslims from Gujarat, drink a lot of soups which they serve in Chinese bowls acquired through India's ancient trade with China. These soups are geared to the seasons. The base for two of them, *sarki*, a summer soup and *sarka* , its winter counterpart, is a split pea – *toovar dal* – that has an ochre colour and an earthy taste. This pulse (legume) is boiled in lots of water. Then, just the water that rises to the top is poured off – as if it were a stock made with bones and meat. It is this split pea stock (broth) that is used. In the summer, cooling vegetables, such as chopped cucumbers and tomatoes are added to it and in the winter, an extraction from ground nuts and seeds, as well as coconut milk.

Here is the summer soup, *sarki*. It is not unlike the Spanish *gazpacho*, only much more interesting, I think. You may serve it with any Indian or Western meal as a first course.

If you cannot get *toovar dal*, use yellow split peas. The broth will have a much sweeter flavour but it will still make a good soup.

METHOD

Put the *dal* or yellow split peas in a pan, along with 3 ¼ pints/ 2 litres/ 8 cups of water and the turmeric. Bring to a boil. Turn heat to low, cover partially and cook for 1 ½ hours or until the *dal* is quite tender. Turn off the heat and let the pan just sit for 5 minutes.

With a ladle, take out all the thin liquid on top of the *dal*. Add enough of the remaining thicker *dal* to make up 2 pints 2 fl oz/ 1.25 litres/ 5 ¼ cups. Put in a blender – you may have to do this in two batches – along with the roasted cumin, lemon juice, salt, black pepper and green chilli. Blend. Taste for seasoning.

Chill for a few hours in the refrigerator. (If allowed to get cold, the soup tends to thicken and jell somewhat. If that happens, stir well before going on with the next step.)

Meanwhile, cut the spring onions (scallions) into 2-in/ 5-cm lengths. Holding several together, cut them into paper-thin rounds. Put in a bowl, cover with cold water and refrigerate for a couple of hours. Drain and dry with absorbent kitchen paper (paper towels).

Drop the tomato into boiling water for 15 seconds. Take it out and peel it. Deseed, if liked. Cut into ¼-in/ 0.5-cm dice as well.

Add the green coriander (Chinese parsley) to the soup and pour into individual bowls. Divide the tomato, cucumbers and spring onions (scallions) among the soup bowls and top with a dollop of yoghurt.

Dahi Shorba

HOT YOGHURT SOUP

SERVES 4

¾ pint/ 2 cups/
450 ml plain yoghurt

3 tbs/ 45 ml chickpea
flour (gram flour/ *besan*)

2 tsp/ 10 ml sugar

¾–1 tsp/ 4–5 ml salt

2 oz/ 50 g, 3–4 nice, firm
radishes, trimmed

2 tsp/ 10 ml vegetable
oil

⅛ tsp ground asafetida

1 tsp/ 5 ml whole black
mustard seeds

1 tsp/ 5 ml whole cumin
seeds

1 tsp/ 5 ml whole
coriander seeds

6-8 curry leaves, fresh or
dried

4 whole, dried hot red
chillies

4 cloves garlic, peeled
and chopped

4 peeled slices of
ginger, finely chopped
(about 1 ½ tsp/ 7 ml)

The Taj Mahal Hotel in Bombay is perhaps India's finest hotel. It is one that I have stayed in since my childhood and watched both interiors and menus change over the years. This yoghurt soup is a relatively new – and very pleasant – addition. It draws its inspiration from similar dishes found in the regions of Gujarat and Maharashtra.

METHOD

Put the yoghurt into a bowl. Beat lightly with a fork or a whisk until smooth.

Put the chickpea flour in a bowl. Slowly add ¾ pint/ 450 ml/ 2 cups of water, mixing well as you do so. (Put through a strainer if lumps form.) Now add the yoghurt to the chickpea flour mixture with the sugar, salt, and whole radishes. Mix and pour into a pan. Bring to a boil over moderate heat. Turn heat down and simmer, uncovered, for 10 minutes. Remove the radishes and set aside.

Organize all your spices for the next step, which goes very fast. Heat the oil in a small frying pan over a medium flame. When hot, put in, first the asafetida, then, a second later, the mustard seeds, cumin seeds and the coriander seeds. When the mustard seeds begin to pop, put in the curry leaves and whole red chillies. As soon as the red chillies start to darken, put in the chopped garlic and ginger. Stir until the garlic pieces brown a bit. Now put the entire contents of the frying pan into the soup. Continue to simmer the soup with the spices for another 5 minutes.

Strain the soup. Cut the radishes into small dice and add to the soup just before serving.

Tomato Saar

TOMATO WITH COCONUT MILK

SERVES 4

S aars are not exactly soups. They *are* soupy, however, and are eaten – in Maharashtra – with Indian breads or rice dishes, accompanied by meats and vegetables. Generally, they are served in small, individual bowls. You could put a spoon in the bowl, if you so choose.

METHOD

Drop the tomatoes into boiling water for 15 seconds. Remove and peel. Chop up the tomatoes and put them into a small pan. Bring to a simmer. Cover and simmer for about 15 minutes or until the tomatoes are soft. Put the tomatoes into the container of a food processor or blender. Blend until smooth.

Put the rice flour in a bowl. Slowly add 8 fl oz/ 250 ml/ 1 cup of coconut milk, mixing as you go, to avoid lumps. Put this liquid into a food processor or blender and blend with the tomatoes.

Heat the oil in a medium-sized pan over a medium flame. When hot, put in first the cumin seeds and, about 30 seconds later, the green chillies. Stir once. Now put in the tomato mixture, the red chilli powder (cayenne pepper), salt, sugar and black pepper. Stir and bring to a simmer. Cook, uncovered, on a low flame for 5 minutes, stirring every now and then. When serving, sprinkle with fresh, green coriander (Chinese parsley).

1 ½ lb/ 700 g, 6 smallish tomatoes

1 tbs/ 15 ml rice flour

8 fl oz/ 250 ml/ 1 cup coconut milk (p. 146)

1 tbs/ 15 ml vegetable oil

¼ tsp whole cumin seeds

1 fresh hot, green chilli, very finely chopped

¼ tsp red chilli powder (cayenne pepper)

about ½ tsp/ 2.5 ml salt

⅛ tsp sugar

freshly ground black pepper

1 tbs/ 15 ml finely chopped fresh, green coriander (Chinese parsley)

Shami Kabab

MINCED/GROUND LAMB PATTIES

MAKES 8 PATTIES AND SERVES 4

2 oz/ ⅓ cup/ 50 g skinned *chana dal* or yellow split peas (p. 149)

1 lb/ 450 g minced (ground) lean lamb

10 whole cloves

1 tsp/ 5 ml whole black peppercorns

1 ¾-in/ 2-cm cinnamon stick

6 cardamom pods

3 bay leaves

about 1 ½ tsp/ 2.5 ml salt

1 ½ tsp/ 7.5 ml peeled, finely grated fresh ginger

1 large egg

2 tbs/ 30 ml very finely chopped onion

1 tbs/ 15 ml very finely chopped fresh mint leaves

1 tsp/ 5 ml very finely chopped fresh, hot, green chilli

vegetable oil

I associate *shami kababs* with joyous, festive times. They are often taken on picnics, packed for hunting trips, served with drinks, (when they are made half their normal size) and eaten at grand meals that also include *pullaos* or *biryanis*. At their best, *shamis* should be delicate and crumbly.

METHOD

Soak the *dal* in 8 fl oz/ 250 ml/ 1 cup of water for 2 hours. Put the *dal*, the water it was soaking in, and the minced (ground) lamb into a heavy, preferably non-stick, pan. Add the cloves, peppercorns, cinnamon, cardamon, bay leaves and salt and bring to a boil. Cover, turn the heat to very low and simmer gently for 1 hour. Remove the lid and turn the heat to medium-high. Boil off all the liquid, stirring constantly. The meat must be very dry, with no hint of liquid. Turn off the heat and allow the meat to cool.

Turn the contents of the pan into the container of a food processor. Grind until you have a fine paste. No whole spices should be visible. Add the ginger and egg. Turn the processor on again briefly, just to mix all the ingredients. Taste and add more salt if necessary. The paste will look rather unmanageable at this stage. Do not worry. Put the contents of the processor into a bowl, cover and refrigerate for at least 2 hours or overnight.

Mix together the chopped onion, mint and green chillies. Divide into eight portions.

Divide the meat paste into eight parts. Form smooth balls out of all the parts. Take one ball at a time and make a deep depression in it with your thumb. Stuff one portion of the onion-mint mixture into the depression. Cover up the depression with the paste and flatten the ball into a smooth patty, about 2 ½ in/ 6.5 cm in diameter. Form all the patties this way.

Pour enough oil into a large, heavy, non-stick, frying pan so that it covers the base to a depth of ⅛ in/ 0.5 cm. Heat it over a medium flame. When hot, put in as many patties as will fit in easily and fry for 3-4 minutes on each side or until they are slightly crisp and a medium brown. As they get done, drain them on any absorbent paper. Make all the patties this way.

Arrange the patties in a single layer in a large serving plate. Separate the onion rings and lay them over the patties. Garnish the plate with the sprigs of fresh mint.

For the garnish:

1 onion, cut into paper-thin rounds

fresh mint sprigs (optional)

Bhaja

DELICIOUS FRIED MORSELS

SERVES 4–6

For the batter

2 oz/ ½ cup/
50 g chickpea flour
(gram flour/ *besan*)

2½ oz/ ½ cup/ 65 g rice
flour

¼ tsp bicarbonate of
soda

½ tsp/ 2.5 ml ground
turmeric

½ tsp/ 2.5 ml red chilli
powder (cayenne
pepper)

¾ tsp/ 4 ml salt

1 ½ tbs/ 22 ml white or
blue poppy seeds

vegetable oil, for deep
frying

A first course at many formal Bengali meals consists of rice, *dal* and *bhaja*. A *bhaja* is a fried titbit. It could be fish – or better still, tender fish roe, or it could be a vegetable or an assortment of vegetables. Slices of aubergine (eggplant) or potatoes could be rubbed with a little salt and turmeric and then deep fried. Sometimes the vegetables are dipped into batter before they are deep fried. Batters can vary slightly from house to house and from vegetable to vegetable. My favourite batter, the one in this recipe, uses both rice flour and chickpea flour. You could make a slightly different batter by using all chickpea flour and adding about 1 tsp/ 5 ml of nigella seeds (*kalonji*).

A great many vegetables can be deep fried. My favourites are pumpkin (sweet potato or yam makes a good substitute), onion, cauliflower, pumpkin or courgette (zucchini) flowers, aubergine (eggplant), potato and potato skins. The last, known as *alur khosha bhaja* is simply superb. Bengalis love to eat it on rainy days with *kichri*, a pilaf of rice and split peas. I like to serve them as a first course with a savoury chutney.

Bhajas should be made at the last minute and eaten hot.

METHOD

Put the chickpea flour, rice flour, bicarbonate of soda, turmeric, chilli powder (cayenne pepper) and salt in a bowl. Slowly add about 8 fl oz/ 250 ml/ 1 cup of water to make a thin batter.

Add the poppy seeds to the batter just before you are ready to use it and mix in.

Pour enough oil into a wok, *karhai* or frying pan to come to a depth of 2 in/ 5 cm. Heat the oil on a lowish flame to about 350°F/ 180°C/ gas mark 4.

Cut the vegetables as suggested in the list of ingredients. Dip as many vegetable pieces into the batter as you think will fit in a slightly over-lapping single layer in your wok, *karhai* or frying pan. Make sure they are evenly coated with batter and then slide them into the hot oil. Fry, stirring now and then, for about 7 minutes or until the vegetables are golden on both sides and cooked through. Remove with a slotted spoon and drain well on absorbent kitchen paper (paper towels), changing the paper at least once or twice. Do all vegetables this way. Flowers and spinach leaves should be fried separately as they tend to cook a bit faster.

Vegetables
———

Singly or in a combination of your choice:
———

potato skins: scrub 2 medium-sized potatoes well and pat dry. Peel the skins in strips that are about ¼ in/ 0.5 cm thick, 1 in/ 2.5 cm wide and 2–3 in/ 5–7.5 cm long. The remaining potato may be cut, crosswise, into ¼-in/ 0.5-cm thick slices
———

yam, sweet potato or pumpkin: peel and cut the pumpkin into about 12 strips, each ¼ in/ 0.5 cm thick, 1 in/ 2.5 cm wide and 2–3 in/ 5–7.5 cm long. A medium-sized sweet potato or yam should be peeled and cut into ¼-in/ 0.5-cm thick rounds
———

aubergine (eggplant): cut a third of a medium-sized vegetable into ⅓-in/ 0.7-cm rounds. Cut each round into three long strips
———

about 12 flowers from courgette (zucchini), pumpkin or marrow (squash) vines
———

12 spinach leaves: wash and pat dry the leaves
———

Labdharay Aloo

POTATOES COOKED WITH GINGER

SERVES 6

2 ¼ lb/ 1 kg potatoes

fresh ginger, about 3 in/
7.5 cm × 1 in/ 2.5 cm ×
1 in/ 2.5 cm

12 oz/ 350 g, 2 large
tomatoes

4 tbs/ 60 ml vegetable
oil

½ tsp/ 2.5 ml whole
cumin seeds

¼ tsp nigella seeds
(*kalonji*)

⅛ tsp fenugreek seeds
(*methi*)

¼ tsp ground turmeric

1 tsp/ 5 ml ground cumin
seeds

1 tsp/ 5 ml ground
coriander seeds

¼ tsp or more red chilli
powder (cayenne
pepper)

¾–1 tsp/ 4–5 ml salt

This popular potato dish, eaten at school lunches, picnics and simple home meals, is generally served with a bread, such as deep-fried *pooris*, and a selection of pickles. I like to serve it as an appetizer on top of a bed of dressed lettuce. I have also been known to serve it with pitta bread, yoghurt, a green vegetable and a chicken or meat dish. Those who are cooking Western meals will find that these potatoes taste quite wonderful with simple roast lamb.

METHOD

Boil the potatoes in their skins. Drain them and let them cool. Peel them and cut them into 1-in/ 2.5-cm dice.

Peel the ginger and chop it coarsely. Place it with 4 tbs/ 60 ml of water into the container of a food processor or blender. Blend.

Chop the tomatoes into very small pieces. Heat the oil in a large frying pan, sauté pan or wide-based pan over a medium-high flame. When hot, put in the whole cumin seeds, nigella seeds, and fenugreek seeds. Stir once and put in the paste from the food processor or blender as well as the turmeric. Stir for 1 minute. Add the tomatoes. Continue to stir and cook until the tomatoes have turned paste-like. Add the ground cumin, ground coriander and chilli powder (cayenne pepper). Stir once or twice. Now put in the potatoes, ½ pint/ 300 ml/ 1¼ cups of water and the salt. Mix well and bring to a boil. Turn heat to low, cover, and simmer gently for 15 minutes.

Bhari Hui Bhindi

STUFFED OKRA

T̲he okra is stuffed with coriander, cumin and *amchoor*, a tart, green mango powder. If you cannot find it, sprinkle over 2 tsp/ 10 ml lemon juice for the final 5 minutes of cooking.

METHOD

Rinse off the okra and pat with absorbent kitchen paper (paper towels) until quite dry. Trim the okra by cutting off the bottom tip and the top cone. (I actually prefer to peel the cone, thus leaving a conical shape on the top of the okra pod.)

In a bowl, mix together the coriander, cumin, *amchoor*, chilli powder, salt and black pepper.

One at a time, hold an okra in one hand and with the other make a long slit in it using a sharp knife. The slit should stop at least ¼ in/ 0.5 cm short of the two ends and it should not go right through the pod. Stick a thumb into the slit to keep it open and with the other hand, take generous pinches of the stuffing and push them into the opening. Stuff all the okra this way. There should be just enough stuffing to fill the pods.

Over a medium-high flame, heat the oil in a frying pan that is large enough to hold all the okra in a single layer. (A 10-inch/ 25-cm pan is ideal though one that is a bit smaller will do.) Put in the onion. Stir and fry until the onion just begins to brown. Put the okra in a single layer and turn the heat to medium low. The okra should cook slowly, uncovered. Gently turn the okra pods around until all sides are very lightly browned. This should take about 15 minutes. Cover the pan, turn the heat to low and cook for another 5 minutes.

SERVES 6

¾ lb/ 350 g whole, fresh okra

1 tbs/ 15 ml ground coriander seeds

1 tbs/ 15 ml ground cumin seeds

1 tbs/ 15 ml ground *amchoor* (p. 143) or 2 tsp/ 10 ml lemon juice

¼ tsp red chilli powder (cayenne pepper)

½ tsp/ 2.5 ml salt

freshly ground black pepper

2 oz/ 50 g, 1 small onion, peeled, cut in half lengthwise and then cut crosswise into fine half rings

6 tbs/ 90 ml vegetable oil

Tala Gosht
QUICK KEBABS

SERVES 6

2 lb/900 g boneless lamb meat from the shoulder cut into 1 ¼–1 ½-in/ 3–4-cm cubes

4 tsp/20 ml very finely grated, peeled fresh ginger

2 tsp/10 ml very finely crushed garlic

4 fresh hot green chillies, very finely chopped

½ tsp/2.5 ml red chilli powder (cayenne pepper)

1 ½ tsp/7.5 ml salt

freshly ground black pepper

2 tbs/30 ml vegetable oil

½ tsp/2.5 ml *garam masala* (p. 151)

mint sprigs and wedges of lime or lemon

This dish from Hyderabad is just as easy as it is delicious and cooks in about 15 minutes. There is, however, a marinating period of 2 hours. Hyderabadis often eat it with Flaky Pan Bread or rice, and a tamarind-flavoured *dal*. You could also offer them as cocktail snacks – just stick toothpicks into them and serve them as soon as they come out of the pan!

METHOD

Cut each cube of meat into narrower ¼-in/ 0.5-cm thick pieces. Pound the pieces with a meat mallet or potato masher so that they flatten out slightly.

Combine the ginger, garlic, green chillies, red chilli powder (cayenne pepper) and salt. Rub this mixture into the meat. Grind lots of black pepper over the meat. Rub that in as well. Set the meat aside for 2 hours.

Heat the oil in a large non-stick frying pan over a medium-low flame. Put in all the meat and slowly, bring it to a simmer. Cover and continue to cook on a medium-low heat for about 15 minutes or until the meat is tender. The meat will cook in its own juices. Remove the cover and turn up the heat a bit. Add the *garam masala*. Boil away all the liquid and gently fry the meat so it turns slightly brown. Serve with mint sprigs and lime wedges.

Heddar
—

MUSHROOMS WITH FENNEL AND GINGER

SERVES 4
—

T his very simple mushroom dish from Kashmir may be served with almost any Indian meal. It may also be served cold, as a salad.

METHOD

Wipe the mushrooms with a wet cloth and cut into ¼-in/ 0.5-cm thick slices.

Heat the oil in a frying pan over a medium-high flame. When hot, put in the mushrooms. Stir and fry the mushrooms for about 2 minutes. Add all the other ingredients. Stir and cook until the tomatoes are soft.

12 oz/350 g mushrooms
—

4 tbs/60 ml vegetable oil
—

6 oz/175 g, 2 smallish tomatoes, chopped
—

¼ tsp ground fennel seeds (fennel seeds may be crushed in a mortar or ground in a clean coffee grinder)
—

¼ tsp ground ginger (*sont*)
—

¼ tsp ground turmeric
—

¼ tsp red chilli powder (cayenne pepper)
—

½ tsp salt
—

Baigan Ki Boorani

AUBERGINE/ EGGPLANT WITH A YOGHURT SAUCE

SERVES 3–4

about 1 lb/ 450 g, 1 large aubergine (eggplant)

2 tbs/ 30 ml ground coriander seeds

1½ tsp/ 7.5 ml ground turmeric

9 cloves garlic, peeled and mashed to a pulp – keep one of the mashed garlic cloves separated from the rest

salt

about 9 tbs/ ¾ cup/ 135 ml vegetable oil

6 oz/ 175 g, 2 medium-sized onions, peeled, cut in half lengthwise and then cut crosswise into very fine, even, half rings

8 fl oz/ 1 cup/ 250 ml plain yoghurt

Here is a dish eaten by the aristocratic Muslim families of Bhopal. It combines three things that I love: aubergine (eggplant), garlic – lots of it – and yoghurt. It shows its Afghan/ Persian ancestry by not being the slightest bit hot.

You may serve it with almost any Indian meal. I find that it goes particularly well at a festive meal with Lucknow's Whole Leg of Lamb and Hyderabadi Pilaf of Rice and Split Peas. You should serve some crunchy relish on the side as well, even if it is just slices of cucumbers seasoned with salt, pepper and lemon juice.

METHOD

Cut the aubergine (eggplant), crosswise into ½-in/ 1-cm thick rounds.

Put the coriander seeds, turmeric and 8 of the mashed garlic cloves into a small bowl. Add ¼ tsp of salt and 4 tbs/ 60 ml/ ⅓ cup of water. Mix.

Line 2 dinner plates with absorbent kitchen paper (paper towels) and set aside.

Heat 5 tbs/ 75 ml of the oil in a frying pan, preferably a non-stick one, over a medium-high flame. When hot, put in the onions. Stir and fry until the onions have turned dark brown and crisp. Remove with a slotted spoon and spread out on one of the plates lined with absorbent kitchen paper (paper towels).

Turn the heat down to medium and put in as many aubergine (eggplant) slices as the pan will hold in a single layer. They will suck up the oil. Let one side brown lightly and then turn the slices over. Add another 2 tbs/ 30 ml of oil, dribbling it along the sides of the pan. Brown the second side. Turn the slices over once more, browning the first side more thoroughly. Remove the slices with a slotted spoon and put on the second dinner plate lined with absorbent kitchen paper (paper towels). Put in a second, and, if needed, a third batch of aubergine (eggplant) slices and cook the same way, adding 2 tbs/ 30 ml of oil after turning the aubergine (eggplant) slices over.

Put the coriander seeds, turmeric and garlic mixture into the oil. Stir and fry it for 2 minutes or so. The paste should dry up and the garlic should get properly fried. Now add 2 tbs/ 30 ml of water. Stir once and turn off the heat.

Put the yoghurt in a bowl. Add the 1 remaining mashed garlic clove and ¼ tsp of salt to it. Stir to mix.

When you get ready to eat, sprinkle the aubergine (eggplant) slices with about ¼ tsp of salt and arrange them, in a single layer, in a large serving plate. Spoon some of the coriander spice mixture over each slice, spreading it over the top. Now cover the slices with large dollops of the yoghurt. Crumble the browned onions and scatter them over the yoghurt. Serve at room temperature.

MEAT

Malai Tikka

BEEF CREAM KEBABS

SERVES 4

T hese beef kebabs, eaten by the Muslim Bohris of Gujarat, are unusual, delicately spiced and quite wonderful. Beef is cubed and marinated in, amongst other things, thick cream. It is then dipped in egg and crumbs, skewered and deep fried. I have not bothered to skewer the pieces as I prefer them to brown evenly on all sides.

You may serve these kebabs with an Indian meal or else as part of a simple Western meal with perhaps a salad and potatoes.

METHOD

Cut away and discard heavy edgings of fat from the meat, if there are any. Cut the steak into 1-in/ 2.5-cm cubes and put in a bowl. Add the ginger, garlic, green chilli, cream and salt. Mix well. Cover and refrigerate for at least 3 hours or overnight.

Just before you are ready to eat, pour enough oil into a wok, *karhai* or deep frying pan to come to a depth of 2 in/ 5 cm. Set to heat over a medium-low flame.

Meanwhile, put the egg into a shallow dish and beat lightly. Put the breadcrumbs in a second, similar dish. Dip the meat cubes, one at a time, first in the egg and then in the crumbs, rolling them around until they are quite encrusted.

When the oil is heated, put in as many meat cubes as the vessel will hold in a single layer. Stir and fry until they are nicely browned on the outside and done to your taste inside. It takes about 4 minutes of frying on a medium-low heat for the meat cubes to be the way I like them – just lightly pink inside. (Most Indians have them well-done.)

1 ½ lb/ 700 g, 1-in/ 2.5-cm thick sirloin steak

2 tsp/ 10 ml very finely grated, peeled fresh ginger

1 tsp/ 5 ml very finely crushed garlic

1–2 tsp/ 5–10 ml very finely chopped (minced) fresh hot green chilli

4 tbs/ ⅓ cup/ 60 ml double cream (heavy cream)

¾ tsp/ 4 ml salt

vegetable oil for deep frying

1 large egg

3 oz/ 75 g/ 1 cup dried breadcrumbs

Do Piaza

LAMB WITH ONIONS AND MINT

SERVES 6

2 lb/ 900 g boned meat from lamb shoulder, cut into 1-in/ 2.5-cm cubes

1 lb/ 450 g, 5 medium-sized onions

2 tsp/ 10 ml salt

1 tsp/ 5 ml red chilli powder (cayenne pepper)

2 tsp/ 10 ml finely grated fresh ginger

1 tsp/ 5 ml finely crushed garlic

1 tsp/ 5 ml ground turmeric

3 tbs/ 45 ml vegetable oil

fresh green coriander (Chinese parsley) to pack a glass measuring jug to the 4 fl oz/ 125 ml/ ½ cup mark

mint to pack a glass measuring jug to the 4 fl oz/ 125 ml/ ½ cup mark

6 fresh hot green chillies, coarsely chopped

3 tbs/ 45 ml lemon juice

A stew-like Hyderabadi dish, this tastes of the sweetness of onions that have simmered for a long time and the freshness of lemon, mint and fresh coriander. It goes well with Hyderabadi Pilaf of Rice and Split Peas and Carrots with Dill.

METHOD

Peel the onions, and cut them in half lengthwise, then crosswise into fine rings. Combine the meat, onions, salt, chilli powder (cayenne pepper), ginger, garlic, turmeric, vegetable oil and ¾ pint/ 400 ml/ 2 cups of water in a wide-based pan. Bring to a simmer. Cover, lower the heat and simmer gently for about 1 hour. Remove the lid, turn up the heat and boil down the sauce until it is very thick.

While the meat is cooking, put the green coriander, mint, green chillies, lemon juice and 2 tbs/ 30 ml of water in the container of a food processor or blender. Blend until as smooth as possible.

When the meat sauce has reduced, pour the contents of the food processor or blender into the pan with the meat. Bring to a simmer. Stir and simmer gently for 3-4 minutes.

Mangsho Jhol

LAMB COOKED WITH ONIONS AND POTATOES

T his simple lamb dish may be served with rice or Indian breads.

METHOD

Put the lamb in a bowl. Add the turmeric, cumin, coriander, red chilli powder (cayenne pepper), ginger and garlic. Mix well, cover and set aside for 2–3 hours.

Peel the onions, and cut them in half lengthwise, then crosswise into rings. Heat the oil in a wide, heavy-based pan over a medium-high flame. Let it get smokingly hot. Now scatter in the sugar. Immediately, put in the onions. Stir and fry the onions until they get a rich brownish colour. Add the meat. Stir and fry the meat for about 10 minutes or until it browns lightly. Now put in the potatoes. Stir and fry them for about 5 minutes. Now put in the salt and ½ pint/ 300 ml/ 1 ¼ cups of water and bring to a boil. Cover, lower the heat and simmer gently for about 1 hour and 10 minutes or until the meat is tender. Stir gently once or twice during this cooking period. Add the *garam masala* and stir.

SERVES 6

1 ¾ lb/ 800 g boned lamb meat from the shoulder, cut into 1 ½-in/ 4-cm cubes

1 tsp/ 5 ml ground turmeric

1 tsp/ 5 ml ground cumin seeds

1 tsp/ 5 ml ground coriander seeds

¼–1 tsp red chilli powder (cayenne pepper)

1 tbs/ 15 ml finely ground, peeled fresh ginger

1 tsp/ 5 ml crushed garlic

1 lb/ 450 g, 4 large onions

4 fl oz/ ½ cup/ 125 ml mustard or vegetable oil

1 tbs/ 15 ml sugar

1 lb/ 450 g, 4 medium-sized potatoes, peeled and quartered

1 ¾ tsp/ 9 ml salt

¾ tsp/ 4 ml Bengali *garam masala* (p. 151)

Marzwangan Korma

LAMB WITH KASHMIRI RED CHILLIES

SERVES 6

1 oz/ 25 g, a walnut-
sized ball of tamarind
(p. 155)

3 lb/ 1.4 kg lamb meat
cut from the shoulder
with bone or 2 ½ lb/
1.1 kg meat from the
shoulder without bone,
cut into 1 ½-in/
4-cm cubes

½ tsp/ 2.5 ml ground
turmeric

1 ¼ tsp/ 6 ml salt

2 tbs/ 30 ml bright red
paprika

½ tsp/ 2.5 ml red chilli
powder (cayenne
pepper)

½ tsp/ 2.5 ml ground
fennel seeds (the seeds
may be finely crushed in
a mortar or ground in a
clean coffee grinder)

½ tsp/ 2.5 ml ground
ginger (*sont*)

5 tbs/ 75 ml
vegetable oil

3 whole cardamom pods

1 ½-in/ 4-cm cinnamon
stick

The traditional recipe for this Kashmiri dish involves deseeding, soaking and puréeing 20 of Kashmir's famous long red chillies. Since those mildly hot chillies are unavailable outside Kashmir, I have substituted a paste made from paprika and red chilli powder (cayenne pepper). Good quality Hungarian paprika gives the same red colouring to foods that Kashmiri chillies do.

This *korma* should be served with Plain Rice and any green vegetable out of this book. At Kashmiri banquets, both this dish and Lamb with Fresh Green Coriander are served, one red and hot, the other pale and mild.

METHOD

Break the tamarind lump up into smaller pieces and put in a small bowl. Add 4 fl oz/ 125 ml/ ½ cup of boiling water and leave to soak for 1 hour. Rub the tamarind pieces with your fingers to release their pulp. Set a strainer over a clean bowl and empty the contents of the bowl containing the tamarind into it. Push out as much pulp as possible.

Put the meat in a pan along with the turmeric, salt, and 1 ¼ pints/ 750 ml/ 3 cups of water. Bring to a boil. Cover, lower the heat and simmer for 50-60 minutes or until the meat is almost tender. Strain the meat and save the stock (broth).

Put the paprika, chilli powder (cayenne pepper), fennel seeds, and ground ginger into a small bowl. Add 4 tbs/ 60 ml of water and work to a smooth paste.

Heat the oil in a wide, heavy-based pan over a

medium flame. When hot, put in the cardamom and cinnamon, the paprika paste and the tamarind paste. Stir and fry until the paste is so well reduced that you can see oil around its edges. Now put in the pieces of meat. Stir and fry them for 3–4 minutes. Now put in all the stock (broth). Stir well and turn the heat up to medium-high. Continue to stir until the stock (broth) is greatly reduced. It should come just about a quarter of the way up the meat.

Before serving, spoon off some of the fat.

Kolhapuri Mutton

LAMB COOKED IN THE KOLHAPURI STYLE

SERVES 4–6

2 lb/ 900 g boned lamb
from the shoulder, cut
into 1½-in/ 4-cm cubes

For the marinade:

4 tbs/ 60 ml plain
yoghurt

2 tsp/ 10 ml very finely
grated peeled fresh
ginger

1 tsp/ 5 ml finely crushed
garlic

¼ tsp turmeric

W ithin Maharashtra, as in much of India, districts, even towns, have their own distinct cuisines. Kolhapur is associated with the foods of the Mahrattas, who were once the bravest of Indian warriors, fighting both Moghul emperors and imperial British forces with great success.

This dish, with its superb, dark sauce, is quite fiery if eaten in Kolhapur. The recipe calls for 10–12 whole red chillies. I find 4 chillies fiery enough. You can use more or less as you desire.

You may serve this meat with rice and any Indian bread. A relish, such as Cucumbers with Fresh Coconut or Tomato and Onion with Yoghurt, could be served on the side.

METHOD

Put the meat in a bowl. Add all the marinating seasonings and mix well. Cover and refrigerate for 3 hours or overnight if you prefer.

Lightly grease a small cast-iron frying pan with ½ tsp/ 2.5 ml of the vegetable oil and heat it over a medium-low flame. When it is hot, put in the dried hot red chillies and the cinnamon stick. Stir these around until the red chillies darken. Remove the spices and put them in a plate. Put the whole cloves, cardamom pods and coriander seeds into the same frying pan. Stir and roast the seeds until they darken a few shades. You will be able to smell the roasted coriander seeds. Put these spices into the same plate as the chillies and cinnamon.

Put all the roasted spices from the plate into the container of a clean coffee grinder or other spice grinder. Grind as finely as possible.

Cut all the onions in half, lengthwise. Now slice half of these sections crosswise into very fine half rings. Chop up the other half as finely as you can.

When the meat has finished marinating, heat the 6 tbs/ 90 ml/ ½ cup of oil in a wide, heavy pan over a medium-high flame. When hot, put in just the sliced onions. Stir and fry them until they are reddish-brown in colour. Now put in the very finely chopped onions and stir them for 1 minute. Turn the heat down to medium-low. Put in the 2 tsp/ 10 ml of garlic and 1 tsp/ 5 ml of ginger. Stir for a few seconds. Put in the ground spices from the coffee grinder and stir once. Now add 4 fl oz/ 125 ml/ ½ cup of water. Continue to cook on a medium-low flame, stirring as you do so, for 3-4 minutes. You will begin to see the oil as it separates from the spice mixture.

Now put in the marinated meat. Turn up the heat to medium-high. Stir and fry the meat with the spice paste for 10 minutes. Add the tomatoes and salt. Continue to stir and cook for another 5 minutes. Now add about 8 fl oz/ 250 ml/ 1 cup of water and bring to a simmer. Cover, turn heat to low and simmer for about 1 hour or until the meat is tender.

Just before serving, you can spoon the fat off the top if you so desire.

For the sauce:

½ tsp/ 2.5 ml vegetable oil

2–4 dried, hot, red chillies

1 ½-in/ 4-cm cinnamon stick

10 whole cloves

10 whole cardamom pods

2 tbs/ 30 ml whole coriander seeds

10 oz/ 350 g, 3 medium-sized onions, peeled

6 tbs/ 90 ml vegetable oil

2 tsp/ 10 ml very finely crushed garlic

1 tsp/ 5 ml very finely grated peeled fresh ginger

½ lb/ 225 g, 3 small tomatoes, very finely chopped

about 1 ¼ tsp/ 6 ml salt

Dhaniwal Korma

LAMB OR CHICKEN WITH FRESH GREEN CORIANDER

SERVES 6

3 lb/ 1.4 kg lamb meat taken from the shoulder with bone cut into 1½-in/ 4-cm cubes or 2½ lb/ 1.1 kg lamb meat from the shoulder without bone, cut into 1½-in/ 4-cm cubes

½ tsp/ 2.5 ml ground turmeric

1¼ tsp/ 7 ml salt

2 large, black cardamom pods (optional)

5 tbs/ 75 ml vegetable oil

7 oz/ 200 g, 2 medium-size onions, peeled, cut in half lengthwise and then cut crosswise into fine half rings

3 whole cloves

5 whole black peppercorns

3 cardamom pods

1½-in/ 4-cm cinnamon stick

This exquisite dish from Kashmir is not the slightest bit hot – it is not meant to be. Meat here is cooked gently in a yoghurt sauce flecked and flavoured with lots of fresh green coriander.

You need rather a lot of coriander. It is hard to tell you exactly how much to buy as it is sometimes sold with roots (which makes it weigh more) and sometimes without. After cutting off the roots and coarse lower stems, the coriander I bought weighed about 7 oz/ 200 g.

Dhaniwal Korma is generally served with Plain Rice. You may serve other Kashmiri vegetables with it or vegetables from almost any other part of India.

This *korma* can also be made with chicken. Cook 3 lb/ 1.4 kg of jointed chicken just the same way as the lamb but reduce the initial boiling time to about 20 minutes or even a bit less if the chicken pieces are very small and tender.

METHOD

Put the meat into a pan along with the turmeric, salt, large black cardamom pods and 1¼ pints/ 750 ml/ 3 cups of water. Bring to a boil. Cover, turn the heat to low and simmer for about 50-60 minutes or until the meat is almost tender.

Heat the oil in a heavy, wide-based pan over a medium-high flame. Put in the onions. Stir and fry them, lowering the heat a bit as they darken, until they are a reddish brown colour and crisp. Remove the onions with a slotted spoon and spread them out in a plate lined with absorbent kitchen paper (paper towels). Leave behind as much oil as possible.

Put the cloves, peppercorns, cardamom pods and cinnamon into the same oil. Stir once and put in all the yoghurt and the garlic. Turn the heat back up to medium-high. Keep stirring the mixture until it has reduced to a very thick, white sauce. Oil should begin to show through along its edges.

When the meat is almost tender, strain it. Save the stock (broth). Add the meat pieces to the yoghurt sauce. Stir and cook the meat over a medium heat for 3–4 minutes. The white sauce should now cling to the pieces of meat. It might even turn golden in spots. Now put in all the stock (broth). Continue to stir and cook until the stock (broth) is reduced and comes about a third of the way up the meat. Crumble the onions and sprinkle them over the meat. Mix in some freshly ground black pepper. Put in all the chopped green coriander (Chinese parsley) just before you serve and stir it in.

Note: the large whole spices in the dish are not meant to be eaten. Also, you will notice a lot of fat floating around the sauce. It should be spooned off just before you serve.

2 pints/ 1.1 litres/ 4 cups plain yoghurt, preferably made from whole milk, lightly beaten with a fork or whisk

———

5 cloves garlic, peeled and crushed

———

freshly ground black pepper

———

enough fresh green coriander (Chinese parsley) to fill a measuring jug to the ¾ pint/ 450 ml/ 2 cup mark after it has had its coarse stems removed, been washed and finely chopped

———

Lucknavi Raan

LUCKNOW'S WHOLE LEG OF LAMB

SERVES 4–6

5-lb/ 2.3-kg leg of lamb
with the H-bone
removed or 5-lb/ 2.3-kg
from the slimmer half of
a very large 8–9-lbs/
3.6–4-kg leg of lamb

2 tsp/ 10 ml meat
tenderizer mixed with
4 tbs/ 60 ml/ ¼ cup
plain yoghurt

2 tbs/ 30 ml whole
cumin seeds

2 tbs/ 30 ml whole white
poppy seeds or
blanched, slivered
almonds

1 oz/ 25 g/ 3 tbs
chickpea flour
(gram flour/ *besan*)

1 whole nutmeg, lightly
crushed

2-in/ 5-cm cinnamon
stick, broken up

9 whole cardamom pods

1 tbs/ 15 ml black
peppercorns

1 ½ tsp/ 7.5 ml whole
cloves

1 ½ tsp/ 7.5 ml whole
mace

Many of the meats in North India are tenderized with green papaya before they are cooked. This gives them a soft and uniquely Indian texture. In my effort to try and get the same texture, I discovered that an 'all natural' meat tenderizer found in US supermarkets contains papain from the papaya fruit. It contains salt as well, which works quite well for this recipe as the meat is supposed to be rubbed with both green papaya and salt at the same time.

If you happen to have a papaya tree and want to use its fruit for this recipe, pick a small 3–4-in/ 7.5–10-cm long, *unripe*, hard green fruit and use about half of it, skin and all, ground up first in a blender or food processor.

Rather like a pot roast, this leg may be served with rice, potatoes and vegetables, or with Flaky Oven Bread, vegetables and relishes.

METHOD

Trim off all the outside fat from the leg and cut or pull off the parchment-like fell that covers some of it. Cut many deep gashes in the meat – about ½-in/ 1-cm apart – with the point of a sharp knife, and then push the meat tenderizer-yoghurt mixture deep into these gashes. Cover the leg with the same mixture and set aside for 30 minutes to 1 hour.

Meanwhile, put the cumin seeds into a small, cast-iron frying pan over a medium flame. Stir and roast the seeds until they are a shade darker and give off a lovely, roasted aroma. Put the seeds into the container of a clean coffee grinder or other spice grinder and grind as finely as possible.

Empty into a large bowl.

Put the poppy seeds into the same frying pan and roast in the same way as the cumin seeds. Grind also and put with the ground cumin seeds.

Put the chickpea flour into the same frying pan. Stir and roast over a medium-low flame until pale brown in colour. Put with the ground seeds.

Now put the nutmeg, cinnamon, cardamom pods, black peppercorns, cloves, mace, large black cardamom pods and red chillies into the coffee grinder or other spice grinder. Grind as finely as possible. Empty into the bowl with the other seasonings. Add the yoghurt and the paprika to the spices as well and mix. Rest the leg of lamb in the bowl and stuff as much of the spice mixture as is possible into the gashes. Cover the leg with the remaining spice mixture and set aside, covered, for 3–4 hours.

Heat the oil in a heavy-based pan (that is large enough to hold the meat) over a medium flame. When hot, put in the onions. Stir and fry until brown. Then put in the leg and all the spice mixture. Let the leg brown lightly on one side. Then turn it over using two kitchen spoons and brown the second side. The sauce will stick to the bottom of the pan. There is no avoiding this. Patiently scrape it off with a spatula and keep frying. When the oil separates from the spices and the leg is lightly browned, add 12 fl oz/ 350 ml/ 1½ cups of water and bring to a simmer. Scrape loose whatever is stuck to the bottom of the pan and mix it in. Cover tightly and cook for about 50 minutes, turning the leg over a few times during this cooking period. The meat should be quite tender by now. Remove the cover and, over the next 10–15 minutes, boil away enough of the liquid to leave you with a thick sauce.

When you get ready to serve, lift the leg out of the sauce and place it in the centre of a platter. Spoon the sauce over the meat, leaving all of the oil behind.

4–5 whole, large black cardamon pods (omit if unavailable)

5–6 whole dried hot red chillies (use more or less, as desired)

¾ pint/ 450 ml/ 2 cups plain yoghurt

1 tbs/ 15 ml bright red paprika

good ¼ pint/ good 150 ml/ good ⅔ cup vegetable oil

8 oz/ 225 g, 2 large onions, peeled, halved lengthwise and cut into very fine half rings

Pakay Gosht Ke Kebab

SKEWERED LAMB KEBABS MADE WITH COOKED MEAT

SERVES 6

8 fl oz/ 1 cup/ 250 ml
plain yoghurt

2 tbs/ 30 ml ground
coriander seeds

2 tsp/ 10 ml peeled and
very finely grated fresh
ginger

½ tsp/ 2.5 ml red chilli
powder (cayenne
pepper)

2 tbs/ 30 ml lemon juice

2 tbs/ 30 ml vegetable
oil

1 tsp/ 5 ml salt

2 ½ lb/ 1 kg boned lean
meat from lamb
shoulder or from lamb
shoulder chops, cut into
2-in/ 5-cm × 1-in/
2.5-cm pieces

8 oz/ 225 g, 2 large
onions, peeled and very
finely chopped

½ tsp/ 2.5 ml ground
turmeric

½ tsp/ 2.5 ml *garam
masala* (p. 151)

Traditionally, all of Delhi's cubed meat kebabs – what the world calls 'shish kebabs' – are made not with raw meat but with meat that has been partially cooked first. This way, the meat gets very tender (it never remains rare, something most Delhi-wallahs would not care for) and the flavour of the spices gets all the way inside.

Once the meat has been partially cooked, you have two options. You could skewer it and brown it over live charcoal – ideal to do in the summer – or you could spread the meat out on a grilling (broiling) tray and brown it under your kitchen grill (broiler).

These kebabs may be served with Indian or Middle Eastern breads or with rice. They should be accompanied by vegetables, salads and yoghurt dishes.

METHOD

Put half the yoghurt, the ground coriander, ginger, chilli powder (cayenne pepper), lemon juice, oil and salt in a large bowl. Beat lightly with a fork or a whisk until smooth and creamy. Add the meat and the onion to the bowl and mix well. Set aside to marinate for 1 hour.

Put the remaining yoghurt into a wide, heavy-based pan. Add the turmeric and *garam masala* and beat lightly with a fork or a whisk until the yoghurt is smooth and creamy. Add the contents of the meat bowl to the pan. Mix. Now bring the meat to a simmer slowly on a medium flame. Cover, turn the heat to low and cook for 30–40 minutes or until the meat is almost, but not quite, done.

Remove the lid, turn up the heat and boil away most of the liquid. Only a thick sauce should cling to the pieces of meat.

If you wish to grill (broil) the meat over charcoal, heat your barbecue. Skewer the meat pieces, about 6 to a skewer, and place over not too hot a fire. Turn the skewer frequently so the meat just gets lightly browned. It should not get charred.

If you wish to brown the meat indoors in your kitchen, light your grill (broiler). If you can control the heat, try not to make it fiercely hot. Spread the meat pieces out in a single layer in a grilling (broiling) tray. Brown the meat on one side then turn the pieces over and do the other side.

POULTRY AND EGGS

Koli Uppu Varuval

CHETTINAD FRIED CHICKEN

This particular quick-cooking, stir-fried dish is made by the Chettiyar community of Tamil Nadu. It is best cooked in a wok or *karhai*, though a frying pan would do.

METHOD

Cut the chicken, with skin, into small serving pieces as one might for Chinese food. (Wings, back, neck and innards may be used for other purposes or frozen for making stock.) The breast should first be split in half. Each half should be cut into 6–8 pieces. Thighs should be halved. So should drumsticks. A heavy cleaver will do the job. Rub ¾ tsp/ 4 ml of the salt and the turmeric on the chicken and set aside for 15 minutes.

Put the remaining ¼ tsp of salt in a bowl with 3 tbs/ 45 ml of water and set aside.

Heat the oil in a wok or *karhai* over a medium-high flame. When hot, put in the mustard seeds. As soon as the mustard seeds begin to pop (this takes just a few seconds), put in the *dal*. As soon as the *dal* turns red, put in the fennel seeds and the red chillies. When the red chillies start to darken, put in the chopped onion. Stir and fry the onion until it browns lightly. Now put in the chicken pieces. Stir and fry the chicken for about 5 minutes. Start sprinkling a little salted water at a time from the bowl over the chicken and keep stirring and frying on a medium-high flame. Fry the chicken for about 10–13 minutes. All the salt water should be used up, and the chicken should be cooked through and slightly browned. Take the chicken out of the oil with a slotted spoon and serve.

SERVES 4

3 lb/ 1.4 kg chicken

1 tsp/ 5 ml salt

¼ tsp ground turmeric

4 tbs/ 60 ml/ ⅓ cup vegetable oil

½ tsp/ 2.5 ml whole black mustard seeds

½ tsp/ 2.5 ml skinned *urad dal* (p. 150)

½ tsp/ 2.5 ml whole fennel seeds

5 whole dried hot red chillies

3 oz/ 75 g, 1 medium-sized onion, peeled and chopped

Arooq

MINCED/GROUND CHICKEN FRITTERS

SERVES 4

2 spring onions
(scallions)

1 lb/ 450 g raw minced
(ground) chicken (I use
raw minced/ ground
boneless chicken breast)

⅛ tsp ground turmeric

¼ tsp red chilli powder
(cayenne pepper)

½ tsp/ 2.5 ml very finely
chopped (minced) fresh,
hot green chilli

½ tsp/ 2.5 ml salt

freshly ground black
pepper

2 tbs/ 30 ml plain white
flour

2 eggs, beaten

vegetable oil, for deep
frying

This dish comes from a family of Iraqi Jews who settled in India over 100 years ago. The *arooq*, an Iraqi dish, has, what with the green chillies and turmeric in it, been Bombayized. It is quite delicious and is the sort of thing that one just cannot stop eating. Amongst Bombay's Iraqi Jews, it is sometimes served with rice and a *dal*. When children come home starving after a day in school, it is stuffed inside a pitta-like bread, along with a little chopped letuce and tomato and served as a snack. I like it best when it just comes out of the wok, either plain or with a mint or fresh coriander chutney acting as a dip. My husband loves it with a generous squeeze of lemon juice. You may also serve it as an appetizer with a savoury chutney.

As the fritters are deep-fried, I find a wok or Indian *karhai* the best utensil to use for the cooking. If you do not have a wok, a frying pan will do. *Arooq* can also be made with minced (ground) fish or very finely minced (ground) lamb.

METHOD

Cut off 1 in/ 2.5 cm of the white, onion-like part of the spring onion (scallion) as well as the top, very green section. You do not need them. Cut the middle sections in half, lengthwise, and then cut these strips crosswise as finely as possible.

Put the minced (ground) chicken in a bowl. Add the turmeric, chilli powder (cayenne pepper), green chilli, salt, black pepper, spring onions (scallions) and flour. Mix well. Add the eggs and mix again. Cover and refrigerate for a least 1 hour. (You can even make the mixture a day ahead of time.)

Just before you are ready to eat, pour enough oil into a wok or *karhai* to come to a depth of 2 in/ 5 cm. Heat the oil over a lowish flame. Give it time to heat.

Use two soupspoons to make the fritters. Lift up a ball of the chicken mixture, about 1 in/ 2.5 cm in diameter, on the front end of one of the spoons. Help release it into the hot oil with the second spoon. Make as many balls as will fit easily in one layer. Stir and fry them until they are golden brown on the outside and cooked inside. This should take about 5 minutes. Adjust your heat, if necessary. Take the fritters out with a slotted spoon and drain on absorbent kitchen paper (paper towels). Make all the fritters this way. Serve them hot.

GREEN CHILLI CHICKEN

SERVES 4
—

3 lb/ 1.4 kg chicken, skinned and cut into small serving pieces
—
1 oz/ 25 g, a walnut of tamarind or 2 tbs/ 30 ml lemon juice
—
1 tsp/ 5 ml salt
—
1 ½ tsp/ 7.5 ml sugar
—
12–15 fresh or dried curry leaves
—
½ lb/ 2 cups/ 225 g shallots, peeled and finely sliced
—
6–7 cloves garlic, finely chopped
—
1 ½-in/ 4-cm cube fresh ginger, peeled and finely chopped
—
7 fresh, hot green chillies, 5 cut into fine rings and 2 cut into long slivers
—
6 oz/ 175 g/ 1 cup, 2 small tomatoes, chopped
—
½ tsp/ 2.5 ml ground turmeric
—
¼ – ½ tsp red chilli powder (cayenne pepper)
—

This superb dish comes from the Jewish Community in Cochin, Kerala, where it is often served for the Friday night dinner, accompanied by Plain Rice or slices of bread. I happen to think that it is scrumptious with *appams* as well. I have modified the recipe only to the extent of using fewer green chillies and shallots and less red chilli powder (cayenne pepper). It may be made a day ahead and refrigerated. Its flavour improves as it sits.

Tamarind is sold by most Indian grocers. If you cannot find it, use fresh lemon juice instead and leave out the boiling water.

METHOD

When cutting up the chicken, cut the breasts into 6 pieces and each leg into 3 or 4.

Break up the tamarind into smaller pieces and put in a cup or small bowl. Cover with 4 fl oz/ ½ cup/ 125 ml of boiling water and set aside for 1–2 hours. Mash up the tamarind and then sieve the pulp into another bowl. Discard the leftovers from the sieve. Mix the sieved pulp with a quarter of the salt and all the sugar. Set aside. Over a medium-high flame, heat the oil in a heavy, casserole-type pan. When hot, put in the curry leaves. Let them sizzle for a couple of seconds. Then add the shallots, garlic, ginger and the 5 chillies cut into rings. Stir and fry for 5–6 minutes or until the shallots have browned lightly.

Now put in the tomatoes. Keep stirring and frying for another 4 minutes or until the tomatoes have turned soft and have started to brown. Add the turmeric and chilli powder (cayenne pepper) and give a quick stir. Now put in the chicken and the remaining salt. Give the chicken a stir. Add ½ pint/ 1 ¼ cups/ 300 ml of water and bring to a simmer. Cover tightly, turn the heat to low and cook for 20 minutes. Stir the chicken once during this time.

Add the slivers of green chilli, cover again and cook for another 5 minutes. Remove the lid. Stir the tamarind mixture and pour it in. Stir the chicken gently to mix. Turn the heat to medium and cook, uncovered, for 10 minutes so the sauce can reduce a bit. As it does so, keep spooning the sauce over the top of the chicken. Take care that the chicken does not stick to the bottom of the pan.

Spoon off some of the surplus fat from the top of the dish before you serve it.

Kozhi Shtew

CHICKEN STEW

SERVES 4–5

3 lb/ 1.4 kg chicken, skinned and cut into reasonably small pieces

5 tbs/ 75 ml vegetable oil

1 ½ tsp/ 7.5 ml whole black peppercorns

3 × 4-cm/ 1 ½-in cinnamon sticks

10 whole cloves

8 whole cardamom pods

1 lb/ 450 g, 3 good-sized onions, cut in half lengthwise and then cut crosswise into fine half rings

1 ½-in/ 4-cm piece fresh ginger, peeled, sliced and then cut into fine slivers

1 tbs/ 15 ml flour

6 whole, fresh hot green chillies slit slightly down their centre

1 pint/ 600 ml/ 2 ½ cups thin coconut milk (p. 146)

In Kerala, this superb stew may be made with chicken, goat or lamb and potatoes, hard-boiled eggs and potatoes or with just potatoes. It is soothing and heavenly in all its forms. If you are using tinned coconut milk, it is particularly easy to prepare.

Traditionally, such stews are eaten at breakfast with *appams* – those deliciously spongy pancakes. Plain Rice combines equally well and may be served instead of *appams*. On the side you could serve Moghlai Spinach and Dry Cauliflower.

If this stew tastes very 'Western' in its seasonings – cloves, cinnamon, and black pepper (many people compare it to Irish stew) – remember that these are Kerala's spices, not those of the Western world. They grow in the back gardens of many private homes. In Kerala, these spices are left whole in the stew. They are just pushed to the side of the plate at mealtime. If this seems bothersome to you, then take the spices out of the pan just after you have fried them. Tie them up in a muslin or cheesecloth bundle and drop them back into the stew when you add the thin coconut milk. The bag can be removed when the stew is cooked.

If you wish to substitute lamb for chicken, get stewing lamb with bone preferably from the neck and shoulder. Cook it for about 50 minutes before adding the potatoes and then continue as for Chicken Stew.

METHOD

When cutting up the chicken, cut the breasts into 6 pieces and each leg into 3 or 4.

Over a medium flame, heat 5 tbs/ 75 ml oil in a large, wide-based casserole pan. When hot, put in the peppercorns, cinnamon sticks, cloves and cardamom pods. Stir once and add the onions and ginger. Sauté until the onions are translucent. Put in the flour and stir it around for 30 seconds. Add the green chillies, chicken and thin coconut milk. Bring to a boil. Cover, turn the heat to low and simmer for 10 minutes. Add the potatoes and the salt and stir. Bring to a boil. Cover, turn the heat to low and simmer for 20 minutes or until the chicken and potatoes are tender. Stir in the lime juice.

Heat the coconut oil in a small frying pan over a medium flame. When hot, put in the sliced shallots. Stir and fry the shallots until they are lightly browned. Put in the curry leaves and stir for a second. Pour the contents of the frying pan into the chicken stew. Stir the thick coconut milk and add it to the stew as well. Bring to a simmer, stirring gently all the time. As soon as the first bubbles appear, turn off the heat. (If you reheat the stew, stir it gently so it does not curdle. Turn off the heat when it just begins to bubble.)

1 lb/ 450 g, 3 medium-sized potatoes, peeled and cut lengthwise into 1-in/ 2.5-cm thick 'fingers' ('thick fries')

about 1 ½ tsp/ 7.5 ml salt

1 tbs/ 15 ml lime or lemon juice

1 tbs/ 15 ml coconut or any other vegetable oil

4 tbs/ 60 ml peeled and finely sliced shallots

15 fresh or dried curry leaves

½ pint/ 300 ml/ 1 ¼ cups thick coconut milk (p. 146)

Murgh Methi

CHICKEN IN A GREEN SAUCE

SERVES 4–6

3 lb/ 1.4 kg chicken, cut into serving pieces and skinned or 3 lb/ 1.4 kg chicken pieces, cut into serving pieces and skinned

4 × 2.5-cm/ 1-in cubes fresh ginger, peeled and coarsely chopped

8–10 cloves garlic, peeled

1 tsp/ 5 ml ground turmeric

6 tbs/ 90 ml/ ½ cup vegetable oil

12 oz/ 350 g, 3 large onions, peeled, cut in half lengthwise and then crosswise into fine half rings

½ pint/ 300 ml/ 1 ¼ cups plain yoghurt

1 ¼ – 1 ½ tsp/ 6–7.5 ml salt

This dish from Hyderabad is nothing short of inspired. The only problem with it is that it requires fenugreek greens – or *methi*. Not just ordinary fenugreek leaves, the kind used in the rest of India, but delicate shoots that are just sending out their first budding leaves. It is this fuss and delicacy that is so typical of the Hyderabadis and their food. I have substituted the equally popular dill for the fenugreek greens. The dish remains wonderful and should, perhaps, be called *Murgh Sooa*. You may serve it with rice or Flaky Pan Bread and any vegetable of your choice. Salads or crunchy relishes should be served on the side.

METHOD

Examine the chicken pieces and remove all extra bits of fat. When cutting the chicken into serving pieces, cut the breast into quarters and the legs into half.

Put the ginger, garlic and 4 fl oz/ 125 ml/ ½ cup of water into the container of a food processor or blender. Blend until you have a paste. Add the turmeric and blend to mix.

Heat the oil in a very wide-based pan over a medium-high flame. When hot, put in the onions. Stir and fry them until they brown lightly in a few spots. Now put in the chicken pieces. Stir them around until they also turn golden, with a few brown spots. Put in the ginger-garlic mixture. Stir and cook on a medium-high heat for another 10 minutes or until the ginger-garlic mixture has browned lightly. Now put in the yoghurt and salt. Stir. Scrape up anything that may have stuck to the bottom of the pan. Bring to a simmer. Cover, lower the heat and simmer for about 15 minutes or until the chicken is almost done.

While the chicken is simmering, put the fresh coriander, green chillies and 4 fl oz/ ½ cup/ 125 ml/ of water into the container of a food processor or blender. Blend until smooth.

When the chicken is almost done, remove the lid and turn the heat up to medium. Boil away some of the liquid to thicken the sauce. Now pour in the mixture from the food processor or blender. Stir to mix and then put in all the chopped dill. Simmer for 5 minutes.

Spoon off as much fat as possible before serving.

enough well-packed, chopped, fresh coriander to fill a glass measuring jug to the 8 fl oz/ 1 cup/ 250 ml level

6 fresh, hot green chillies, coarsely chopped

enough well-packed, chopped, fresh dill to fill a glass measuring jug to the 8 fl oz/ 1 cup/ 250 ml level

Sali Jardaloo Murgi

CHICKEN WITH APRICOTS AND POTATO STRAWS

3 lb/ 1.4 kg chicken, or chicken pieces, skinned

4 whole dried hot red chillies

2-in/ 5-cm cinnamon stick, somewhat broken up

1 ½ tsp/ 7 ml whole cumin seeds

7 cardamom pods

10 whole cloves

2 tsp/ 10 ml finely grated peeled, fresh ginger

1 tsp/ 5 ml finely crushed garlic

4 oz/ 100 g/ 15–16 stoned (pitted) dried apricots

6 tbs/ 90 ml/ ½ cup vegetable oil

½ lb/ 225 g, 2 good-sized onions, peeled, cut in half lengthwise and then cut crosswise into very fine half rings

2 tbs/ 30 ml tomato purée (paste) mixed with 8 fl oz/ 1 cup/ 250 ml water

This festive dish is eaten only by the Parsis of Bombay. It combines two of their favourite things – sweet-and-sour foods and potato straws.

METHOD

If using a whole chicken, cut it into small serving pieces. Divide the legs into 2 and the whole breasts into 4 pieces.

Put the red chillies, cinnamon, cumin seeds, cardamom pods and cloves into the container of a coffee grinder or other spice grinder. Grind finely.

Put the chicken in a big bowl. Put 1 tsp/ 5 ml of the ginger, ½ tsp/ 2.5 ml of the garlic and half the dry spice mixture on the chicken. Mix well with your hands, rubbing the seasonings into the chicken pieces. Set aside for 1 hour.

Put the apricots in a small pan with ¾ pint/ 2 cups/ 450 ml of water. Bring to a boil. Turn the heat down and simmer, uncovered, until the apricots are tender but not mushy. (The time will vary depending upon the quality of the dried fruit and on whether they are whole or halved.) When the apricots are tender, turn off the heat and let them sit in their own juice.

When the chicken has completed its marinating time, heat the 6 tbs/ 90 ml/ ½ cup of oil in a wide, heavy pan over a medium-high flame. When hot, put in the onions. Stir and fry until they turn a rich, reddish-brown colour. Turn the heat down to medium and add the remaining 1 tsp/ 5 ml of ginger and ½ tsp/ 2.5 ml of garlic. Stir once or twice. Now put in the remaining dry spice mixture from the coffee grinder. Stir once or twice and put in all the chicken. Stir and brown the chicken lightly for 5 minutes. Now put in the tomato purée (paste) liquid and the salt. Bring to a boil. Cover, reduce the heat to low and simmer gently for 20 minutes. Add the vinegar and sugar. Stir to mix. Cover again and simmer for another 10 minutes. Turn off the heat. Spoon off as much fat from the surface as possible.

Put the apricots into the pan with the chicken. (If the apricots were sitting in only a little bit of liquid, say 2–3 tbs/ 30–45 ml put that in as well. If there is more liquid than that, discard it.) Gently slip the apricots in between the chicken pieces and let them soak in the sauce for at least 30 minutes.

Make the potato straws: fill a large bowl with about 3 pints/ 1.75 litres/ 8 cups of water. Add the salt and mix.

Grate the potato on the coarsest grating blade. Put the grated potato into the bowl of water. Stir the potatoes about with your hand. Now remove one handful of potatoes at a time, squeezing out as much liquid as you can. Spread the potatoes out on a tea towel (dish towel). Pat with absorbent kitchen paper (paper towel) to dry off as much moisture as possible.

Pour vegetable oil into a wok, *karhai* or frying pan to a depth of 2 in/ 5 cm. Heat over a lowish heat. Let the oil heat slowly. When it is hot – this may take 10 minutes – put in one smallish handful of the uncooked straws. They will begin to bubble. When the bubbling stops, stir them until they are crisp and a pale golden colour. Remove with a slotted spoon and leave to drain on a plate lined with absorbent kitchen paper (paper towel). Make all the potato straws this way.

When you are ready to eat, heat the chicken gently and put it in a serving dish. Garnish the top with the potato straws.

1 ¼ tsp/ 6 ml salt

2 tbs/ 30 ml distilled white malt vinegar

1 ½ tbs/ 22 ml sugar

For the potato straws (*sali*):

1 tbs/ 15 ml salt

7 oz/ 200 g, 1 large potato, peeled

vegetable oil for deep frying

Moghlai Murgh Dumpukht

MOGHLAI CHICKEN BRAISED WITH ALMONDS AND RAISINS

SERVES 6
—

3 ½ lb/ 1.6 kg chicken, skinned and cut into serving pieces
—

1 tsp/ 5 ml salt
—

freshly ground black pepper
—

2 tbs/ 30 ml vegetable oil
—

2 oz/ 50 g/ 4 tbs unsalted butter
—

7 whole cardamom pods
—

8 whole cloves
—

2-in/ 5-cm cinnamon stick
—

2 bay leaves
—

1 oz/ 25 g/ 2 ½ tbs blanched, slivered almonds
—

1 oz/ 25 g/ 2 ½ tbs raisins or sultanas (golden raisins)
—

8 fl oz/ 1 cup/ 250 ml plain yoghurt
—

1 tsp/ 5 ml ground cumin seeds
—

¼ – ½ tsp red chilli powder (cayenne pepper)
—

W hen in the seventeenth century an English traveller encountered this dish in Moghul India, he referred to it as 'Dumpoked' fowl; this was his way of saying *dumpukht*, the Moghul word for slow braising in a tightly sealed pan. In India today, this word has now been shortened to *dum*. He also described it as fowl 'boiled in butter in any small Vessel and stuffed with Raisins and Almonds'.

This dish is easy to make, mild, and very elegant. It is best served with rice and perhaps Moghlai Spinach.

METHOD

When you cut the chicken into serving pieces divide whole legs into two and whole breasts into six pieces. Spread the chicken pieces out in a single layer and sprinkle with ¼ tsp of salt and some freshly ground black pepper. Pat the salt and pepper in so they adhere. Turn the chicken pieces over and sprinkle with another ¼ tsp of salt and some freshly ground black pepper. Pat this in as well.

Heat the oil and butter in a large, preferably non-stick, frying pan over a medium-high flame. When hot, put in the cardamom, cloves, cinnamon, bay leaves and as many of the chicken pieces as the pan will hold in a single layer. Brown the chicken on both sides. As soon as the pieces get browned, lift them up with a set of tongs or a slotted spoon and put them in an oven-proof, flame-proof, casserole pan. Do all the chicken this way.

Put the almonds into the hot oil left in the

frying pan. Stir them once or twice. As soon as they start to brown, put in the raisins and stir once. Quickly, before the raisins start to burn, pour the contents of the frying pan, fat and all, over the chicken in the casserole pan.

Preheat the oven to 350°F/ 180°C/ gas mark 4.

Put the yoghurt in a bowl. Add the cumin, chilli powder (cayenne pepper) and the remaining ½ tsp/ 2.5 ml of salt as well as some freshly ground black pepper. Beat lightly with a fork or whisk until smooth and creamy. Pour the yoghurt over the chicken and mix well. Cover the pan tightly and place in the oven. Bake for 20 minutes. Turn the chicken pieces over and baste with the juices surrounding them. Cover tightly and return to the oven for another 20–25 minutes or until the chicken is quite tender.

When you are ready to eat, reheat the chicken over a low flame. Lift out the chicken pieces and put them in a warm serving dish. Spoon off most of the fat left in the pan. If the remaining sauce is thin, reduce it by cooking it over a medium-high flame. Pour this thick sauce over the chicken pieces.

Beware! The large, whole spices are not meant to be eaten.

Rajasthani Murgh Ka Soola

RAJASTHANI GRILLED (BROILED) OR BAKED CHICKEN

SERVES 4

2 lb/ 900 g chicken, cut
into serving pieces
(whole legs cut into
2 and whole breasts
into 4)

salt

2 tbs/ 30 ml lemon juice

5 tbs/ 75 ml vegetable
oil

4 oz/ 100 g, 1 large
onion, peeled, cut in
half lengthwise and then
cut crosswise into fine
half rings

8 large cloves garlic,
peeled and sliced
crosswise

3 tbs/ ¼ cup/ 45 ml
slivered, blanched
almonds

2 x 1-in/ 2.5-cm cubes of
fresh ginger, peeled and
coarsely chopped

1 ½ tsp/ 7.5 ml *garam
masala* (p. 151)

4 tbs/ 60 ml/ ⅓ cup
plain yoghurt

½ – ¾ tsp/ 2.5–4 ml red
chilli powder (cayenne
pepper)

In Rajasthan, the men – who have traditionally been warriors – do a great deal of outdoor
cooking, generally of meats which are skewered
and cooked over an open fire. There are many
variations of this particular dish. The one here
happens to be the simplest. I have adapted it so the
cooking can be done without skewers over a charcoal grill or indoors in an oven.

Ideally, the chicken should be marinated
overnight though, at a pinch, 4 hours will do.

You could serve this with Aubergine/ Eggplant
with a Yoghurt Sauce and Bhopali Pilaf with Peas
and Carrots. I sometimes serve it with a plain
green salad.

METHOD

Skin the chicken pieces and spread them out in a
large plate in a single layer. Prick them thoroughly with a tip of a sharp knife and then sprinkle ¼
tsp of salt and 1 tbs/ 15 ml of lemon juice over
them. Turn the pieces over and prick them again
with the knife and sprinkle another ¼ tsp of salt
and 1 tbs/ 15 ml of lemon juice over this second
side. Rub the salt and lemon juice into the flesh.
Put the chicken pieces in a bowl and set aside for
1 hour or more. Turn the chicken pieces over a few
times during this period.

Meanwhile, prepare the second marinade: heat
the oil in a frying pan over a medium-high flame.
When hot, put in the onion and garlic. Stir and fry
until the onion turns reddish-brown in colour.
Turn heat to low as you remove the onion and garlic with a slotted spoon and place in a bowl. Put the

almonds into the same hot oil. Stir and fry for a few seconds until they turn golden brown. Remove with a slotted spoon and put with the onion and garlic. Turn off the heat and save the oil in the pan.

Put the fried onion, garlic and almonds, as well as the ginger and 5 tbs/ 75 ml of water, into the container of a food processor or blender. Blend until you have a smooth paste. Empty into a bowl. Add the *garam masala*, yoghurt, red chilli powder (cayenne pepper) and ½ tsp/ 2.5 ml of salt. Mix. Pour this marinade over the chicken and mix well. Prick the chicken pieces again with the point of a sharp knife, again pushing as much of the marinade into the flesh as possible. Cover the chicken and refrigerate overnight.

To grill (broil) outdoors over charcoal: light the charcoal and let it get ashen-white. Make sure that the grill (broiler) is placed so it is at least 5 in/ 12.5 cm away from the source of heat. Spread the chicken pieces out on the grill (broiler). Extra marinade should be put on top of the pieces. The chicken should cook slowly. Turn the pieces from time to time and cook for about 40 minutes in all. If your grill (broiler) is the type with a cover, you could use it after you have browned the chicken on both sides. Baste the chicken frequently with the oil left over from frying the onion, garlic and almonds.

To bake the chicken in an oven: preheat the oven to 400°F/ 200°C/ gas mark 6. Spread the chicken pieces out in a shallow baking tray in a single layer. Extra marinade can be put on top of the pieces. Dribble half of the oil left over from frying the onion, garlic and almonds over the chicken and put the baking tray in the oven. Bake for 20 minutes. Turn the chicken pieces over. Dribble the remaining oil over the chicken and return it to the oven. Bake for another 20–25 minutes, basting it once or twice with the juices.

Tomato Kut

HYDERABADI EGGS IN A TOMATO SAUCE

SERVES 4

2 lb/ 900 g ripe
tomatoes, chopped
finely

2 tbs/ 30 ml whole
coriander seeds

2 tbs/ 30 ml tamarind
paste (p. 155)

2 tsp/ 10 ml very finely
grated, peeled fresh
ginger

1 clove garlic, mashed to
a pulp

½ tsp/ 2.5 ml red chilli
powder (cayenne
pepper)

20 fresh or dried curry
leaves

2 tbs/ 30 ml chopped,
fresh green coriander
(Chinese parsley)

1 tsp/ 5 ml ground,
roasted cumin seeds
(p. 148)

2 tsp/ 10 ml chickpea
flour (gram flour/ *besan*)

1 tbs/ 15 ml vegetable oil

⅛ tsp whole mustard
seeds

A s the juiciness of tomatoes varies so much, it
is hard to give an exact recipe here. You may
have to make your own adjustments. A *tomato kut*
is a delicately spiced tomato purée which may be
eaten, as is, or may have hard-boiled eggs partially imbedded in it, making it a very useful dish for
breakfasts, brunches and lunches. It goes particularly well with rice though you may also serve it
with toast.

METHOD

Put the tomatoes, coriander seeds, tamarind paste,
ginger, garlic, chilli powder (cayenne pepper), 10
of the curry leaves, and the fresh coriander into a
heavy-based pan. Place on a low flame. Cover.
The tomatoes will begin to release their juices.
Start to simmer and keep simmering gently until
the tomatoes are very soft. Now sieve them into a
bowl. Discard the contents of the sieve. Add the
ground, roasted cumin seeds to the purée and
mix. Rinse out the cooking pan and put the purée
back in it.

Examine your purée. If it is very thin, it might
require more than the 2 tsp/ 10 ml of chickpea
flour. My purée is generally just a little thinner
than the average tomato soup and I have about ¾
pints/ 2 cups/ 450 ml.

Put the chickpea flour in a small cast-iron frying pan over a medium-low flame. Stir it about
until it turns slightly brown. Empty it into a small
bowl and mix with 1 tbs/ 15 ml of water. Add this
mixture to the tomato purée. Bring the purée to a
simmer over a medium-low flame, stirring. Turn

the flame down and let it cook gently for 2–3 minutes.

Heat the oil in a small frying pan. When hot, put in the mustard seeds, whole cumin seeds, fenugreek seeds, nigella seeds, red pepper and remaining 10 curry leaves. As soon as the red pepper begins to darken, put in the garlic. When the garlic browns a little, pour the contents of the frying pan into the pan with the purée.

Put the purée into a serving dish. Cut the hard-boiled eggs in half, crosswise, and arrange them, cut side up, in the serving dish so that they are at least half buried in the purée.

Note: the whole, hot red chilli should be approached with caution.

⅛ tsp whole cumin seeds

2–3 whole fenugreek seeds

⅛ tsp nigella seeds (*kalonji*)

1 whole dried, hot red pepper

1 large clove garlic, cut in quarters, lengthwise

4 hard-boiled eggs, peeled

FISH AND SHELLFISH

Bhopali Hare Masale Ki Macchli

BHOPALI FISH WITH GREEN SEASONINGS

F ish abound in Bhopal's lakes and anglers line the shores on most week-ends and holidays. Here is one simple but tasty way in which the freshly-caught fish is cooked. You may deep-fry it in a wok or *karhai*, or else shallow-fry it in a frying pan, making sure the oil comes at least halfway up the pieces of fish.

SERVES 4

1 ½ lb/ 700 g thick-cut fillets of any firm, white-fleshed fish such as cod, halibut, haddock, scrod or red snapper, or 1 ¾ lb/ 800 g of 'steaks' with bone

salt

2 tbs/ 30 ml lemon juice

3 oz/ 75 g/ about 1 ¼ cups well-packed fresh green coriander (Chinese parsley)

6 fresh hot green chillies

4–6 cloves garlic, peeled

6 fl oz/ ¾ cup/ 175 ml plain yoghurt

vegetable oil for deep or shallow frying (see recipe note above)

METHOD

If you have a large fillet, cut it into pieces that are about 2–2 ½ in/ 5–6.5 cm long and 1 ½ in/ 4 cm wide. Spread the pieces out in a single layer in a large plate and sprinkle with about ⅓ tsp of salt and 1 tbs/ 15 ml of lemon juice. Turn the pieces over and repeat with another ⅓ tsp of salt and 1 tbs/ 15 ml of lemon juice. Set the plate at a tilt and leave it tilted for 2–3 hours. As water accumulates at one end, discard it.

Put the green coriander (Chinese parsley), green chillies, garlic, ¼ tsp of salt and 2 tbs/ 30 ml of water into the container of a food processor or blender. Blend until you have a paste. Empty the paste into a deep dish or shallow bowl. Put the yoghurt into another deep dish or shallow bowl. Add ¼ tsp of salt to the yoghurt and mix it in.

Set the oil to heat in a wok, *karhai* or frying pan over a medium flame. When very hot, dip 2 or 3 pieces of fish, first in the yoghurt and then in the green paste to cover thoroughly and then put them in the hot oil. Fry for about 5 minutes, turning the pieces over once, until the fish is cooked through. Remove with a slotted spoon. Fry all the pieces of fish this way and serve hot.

Chingri Maachher Jhal

PRAWNS/SHRIMPS WITH MUSTARD SEEDS

SERVES 4

1 tbs/ 15 ml whole black mustard seeds

1 tbs/ 15 ml whole yellow mustard seeds (use twice this quantity if you cannot find black mustard seeds)

½ tsp/ 2.5 ml ground turmeric

½ tsp/ 2.5 ml red chilli powder (cayenne pepper)

½ tsp/ 2.5 ml salt

1 lb/ 450 g uncooked prawns (shrimps) with shell but no head (about 13 oz/ 375 g shelled)

4 tbs/ 60 ml mustard oil or vegetable oil

⅓ tsp/ 3 ml nigella seeds (*kalonji*)

4 whole, dried, hot red chillies

3 fresh hot green chillies

F or me, no dish could be more typical of Bengal than this one. It is simple to cook – and yet quite distinctive in the nose-tingling pungency it acquires from the ground mustard seeds in its sauce. In Calcutta, it is cooked only with inland, estuary prawns (shrimps) that are known for their sweetness. Heads are always cooked and are preferred by many diners for their richness and flavour. As prawns (shrimps) with heads are hard to find in the West, I have, reluctantly, left them out.

Serve the dish with Plain Rice. Any *dal* and a vegetable may also be served.

METHOD

Put the black mustard seeds and the yellow mustard seeds into the container of a clean coffee grinder or food processor. Grind. Empty the ground spices into a small bowl. Add the turmeric, red chilli powder (cayenne pepper), salt and 6 tbs/ ½ cup/ 90 ml of water. Mix.

Peel the prawns (shrimps), but leave their tails on. Heat the oil in a frying pan over a medium flame. Let it get smokingly hot for a second, if using mustard oil. Now put in the nigella seeds (*kalonji*) and a second later, the red chillies. Stir once and put in the prawns (shrimps). Stir for 1 minute. The prawns (shrimps) will just start to turn pink. Now put in the mixed spice paste and the green chillies. Stir on a medium heat for 1–2 minutes or until the prawns are just done and the sauce is a bit thicker.

Note: the whole chillies should be eaten only by those who know what they are doing.

Kolumbi Tse Kalvan

PRAWNS/SHRIMPS COOKED IN THE MAHARASHTRIAN MANNER

H ere is a quick dish which you may make with prawns (shrimps) or any firm-fleshed fish that can be cut into thick steaks or chunks. Serve with rice and vegetables such as Stuffed Okra, Carrots with Dill and Puréed Vegetables.

METHOD

If the prawns (shrimps) are unpeeled, peel them. Devein them (p. 154). Put them in a bowl. Add the crushed garlic, ginger, tamarind paste, turmeric, salt and chilli powder (cayenne pepper). Mix well and set aside for 10 minutes (not longer, as raw ginger tends to affect the texture of the prawns/ shrimps).

Peel the whole cloves of garlic, then mash lightly but leave whole. Heat the oil in a frying pan over a medium-high flame. When hot, put in the mashed cloves and stir until they brown lightly. Now put in the prawns (shrimps). Stir for 1 minute so the prawns (shrimps) can also brown lightly. Turn the heat to medium-low. Put in the coconut milk, fresh coriander (Chinese parsley) and green chillies. As soon as the sauce begins to simmer, turn off the heat and serve.

SERVES 4

1 lb/ 450 g medium-sized uncooked prawns (shrimps) unpeeled (but no heads) or 12–13 oz/ 350–375 g peeled, uncooked prawns

1 clove garlic, finely crushed

1 tsp/ 5 ml finely grated, peeled fresh ginger

3 tbs/ 45 ml tamarind paste (p. 155)

⅛ tsp ground turmeric

¾ tsp/ 4 ml salt

¼ tsp hot, red chilli powder (cayenne pepper)

3 cloves garlic

2 tbs/ 30 ml vegetable oil

4 fl oz/ ½ cup/ 125 ml unsweetened coconut milk, tinned or fresh (p. 146)

1 tbs/ 15 ml finely chopped fresh coriander (Chinese parsley)

2 fresh hot green chillies, very finely chopped

Konju Pappaas

PRAWNS/ SHRIMPS COOKED WITH COCONUT MILK

SERVES 6

2 lb/ 900 g unpeeled,
uncooked medium-sized
prawns (shrimps)
without heads or 1 ½ lb/
700 g peeled prawns
(shrimps)

2 tbs/ 30 ml whole
coriander seeds

¼ tsp whole fenugreek
seeds

1 tsp/ 5 ml whole black
peppercorns

10 dried curry leaves
(you do not need these
if fresh ones are
available)

1 tbs/ 15 ml fish
tamarind (*kodampoli*)
cut into slivers the width
of a pencil or 2 tsp/
10 ml lemon juice

5 tbs/ 75 ml vegetable
oil

1 tsp/ 5 ml whole black
mustard seeds

10 fresh curry leaves, if
available

1 medium-sized onion,
peeled, cut into half
lengthwise and then cut
crosswise into half rings

I love this dish from Kerala with a passion.
Give it to me with a bowl of Plain Rice and
I will not ask for anything more.

There are two ingredients here that may be
hard to find. Do not let that stop you from cooking it as I will suggest alternatives. The first ingredient is *kodampoli*, a sour, smoky tamarind that
balances the creamy sweetness of the coconut
milk. Lemon juice may be used in its place. The
second ingredient is fresh curry leaves. If you cannot get them, use the dried ones and leave out
the step that calls for the fresh ones.

I often make this dish when I am entertaining
as most of the work can be done ahead of time. The
sauce can be made and the prawns (shrimps)
peeled well before the guests arrive. Then all I do
5 minutes before we sit down to eat is heat the
sauce, fold the prawns (shrimps) into it so they
cook through and then pour in the coconut milk.

If you want the dish to end up being mildly
hot, use ¾ tsp/ 4 ml of chilli powder (cayenne
pepper). The sauce may taste quite fiery before the
prawns (shrimps) and coconut milk are added
but the final result will be fairly mild.

METHOD

If the prawns (shrimps) are not peeled, peel them.
Devein the prawns (shrimps) (p. 154). Wash them
quickly and pat them dry. Cover and refrigerate.

Heat a small, 5-in/ 12.5-cm, cast-iron frying
pan (a crêpe pan will do) over a medium flame.
When hot, put in the coriander seeds, the fenugreek seeds and the peppercorns. Stir them about

for 1 minute or so until they are lightly roasted. Remove from the heat. Put them into the container of a spice grinder or coffee grinder along with the dried curry leaves (if you are using them). Grind as fine as possible. Wash the fish tamarind slivers (if using them) under running water and then soak them in about half a teacup of water for 5 minutes. Drain. Heat the oil in a 10-in/ 25.5-cm frying pan or in a wide pan over a medium flame. When hot, put in the mustard seeds. As soon as the mustard seeds begin to pop put in the fresh curry leaves, if you are using them. Stir once and put in the onion and garlic. Stir and fry until they are lightly browned. Add the ginger. Stir and cook for another few seconds. Now put in ¾ pint/ 1 ¾ cups/ 450 ml of water, the paprika, red chilli powder (cayenne pepper), turmeric, salt, whole chillies, the ground spice mixture and either the drained fish tamarind or lemon juice. Bring to a boil. Turn the heat to medium-low and simmer vigorously for 5 minutes. Turn off the heat. (This sauce base may now be kept for several hours.)

Five minutes before you want to eat, heat the sauce in the frying pan over a fairly high flame. As soon as it begins to bubble, put in all the prawns (shrimps). Stir them around until they just turn opaque. Stir the coconut milk and pour it in. Keep stirring the contents of the frying pan. When the coconut milk is heated through and the first bubbles begin to appear, turn off the heat and serve.

5 cloves garlic, peeled and cut into fine slivers

1 tsp/ 5 ml peeled and finely grated fresh ginger

2 tbs/ 30 ml bright red paprika

¾ tsp/ 4 ml red chilli powder (cayenne pepper)

½ tsp/ 2.5 ml ground turmeric

about ¾ –1 tsp/ 4–5 ml salt

3 whole fresh, hot green chillies

14 fl oz/ 1 ¾ cups/ 400 ml fresh or tinned, unsweetened coconut milk (p. 146)

Meen Molee

FISH IN A CREAMY SAUCE

SERVES 6

3-in/ 7.5-cm piece of fresh ginger, peeled

6 fresh hot green chillies

7 cloves garlic, peeled

1 tbs/ 15 ml flour

1 ¼ pints/ 3 cups/ 750 ml thin coconut milk (p. 146)

4 tbs/ ⅓ cup/ 60 ml vegetable oil

9 oz/ 250 g/ 3 medium-sized onions, peeled, cut lengthwise into half and then cut crosswise into fine slices

¾ tsp/ 4 ml turmeric

¼ – ½ tsp red chilli powder (cayenne pepper)

about ½ tsp/ 2.5 ml salt

1 lb/ 3 cups/ 450 g/ 3 medium-sized tomatoes, chopped

1 ¾ lb/ 800 g haddock or halibut fillets, cut at least 1 ½ in/ 4 cm thick

½ pint/ 1 ¼ cups/ 300 ml thick coconut milk (p. 146)

T his dish is a favourite at parties in Kerala and is often served with rice or bread. (You could also serve it with a crusty loaf of French or Italian bread.) It is frequently much hotter than I have made it. You can make it more or less hot, according to your taste. In Kerala, the fish that was used for this *molee* was the firm-fleshed seer. Haddock, halibut, cod, scrod, monk fish or bream all make good substitutes. Buy thick fillets or use fish steaks. The choice of cut is crucial as the dish needs thick chunks of fish that won't disintegrate easily. Buy thick fillets or use 'steaks' of fish that have been cut crosswise.

METHOD

Chop 2 in/ 5 cm of the ginger coarsely. Take 3 of the green chillies and chop them coarsely. Put the chopped ginger, chopped green chillies and garlic into a container of a food processor or blender along with 4 tbs/ ⅓ cup/ 60 ml of water. Blend until you have a somewhat coarse paste. Take the remaining 1 in/ 2.5 cm of ginger and cut it crosswise into very fine slices. Stack up the slices, a few at a time and cut into very fine strips.

Cut small slits down the middles of the 3 remaining green chillies. Put the flour in a bowl. Slowly add the thin coconut milk, mixing well as you do so. Strain, if lumps form.

Heat the oil in a large wok or wide pan over a medium flame. When hot, put in the sliced onions, the strips of ginger and the whole, slit green chillies. Stir and fry until the onions just start to brown, this takes about 2 minutes. Now add the paste from the food processor or blender. Stir and fry for about 5 minutes. Add the turmeric and chilli powder (cayenne pepper) and stir once or twice. Now put in the thin coconut milk, salt and tomatoes. Mix and stir gently until the sauce comes to a boil. Let the sauce cook on a medium flame for about 10 minutes or until the tomatoes have softened and the sauce has reduced a bit. Stir as this happens.

Cut the fish into pieces about 2 ½ in/ 6.5 cm square and slip them into the sauce. Turn the heat down a bit to allow the fish to poach gently. Ladle the sauce over the fish as it does so. It should take about 10 minutes to cook through. Pour in the thick coconut milk. As soon as bubbles begin to appear in the sauce, turn off the heat.

Lift the fish pieces carefully out of the pan and put in a serving dish. Pour over the sauce.

Patia

FISH IN A DARK SAUCE

SERVES 4

10 oz/ 275 g, 2 good-sized onions

5 tbs/ 75 ml vegetable oil

2 tsp/ 10 ml very finely grated, peeled fresh ginger

2 tsp/ 10 ml finely crushed garlic

2 tsp/ 10 ml very finely chopped fresh green chillies

2 tsp/ 10 ml ground roasted coriander and cumin seed mixture (p. 148)

½ tsp/ 2.5 ml red chilli pepper (cayenne pepper)

12 oz/ 350 g, 3 small tomatoes

1 tsp/ 5 ml sugar

2 tsp/ 10 ml distilled white malt vinegar or cider vinegar

1 ¼ tsp/ 6 ml salt

1 ½ lb/ 700 g fish steaks, cut about 1 in/ 2.5 cm thick (see recipe note)

Very slightly sweet and sour, this Parsi dish from Bombay is another favourite with our family. We serve it with rice. In India, firm-fleshed pomfrets are used. Unfortunately, they are very difficult to find in the West. You could use chunks of either halibut or haddock, or steaks of bass, pompano or red snapper. I used steaks with bone but boneless fish pieces would work as well. You can also make this dish with prawns (shrimps).

METHOD

Peel the onions, cut them in half lengthwise and then into fine half rings. Heat the oil in a frying pan over a medium-high flame. When hot, put in the sliced onions. Stir and fry them until they are a rich reddish-brown colour. Turn the heat down to medium and put in the ginger and garlic. Stir for ½ minute. Now put in the coriander and cumin seed mixture and the red chilli pepper (cayenne pepper). Stir once or twice. Put in the tomatoes, sugar, vinegar, salt and ½ pint/ 1 ¼ cups/ 300 ml of water. Bring to a boil. Cover, lower the heat and simmer gently for 30 minutes. Remove the cover and put in the fish pieces. Spoon the sauce over the fish and bring to a simmer. Cover and simmer gently for about 15 minutes or until the fish is just done.

Patra Ni Macchi

FISH IN A PACKET

SERVES 4

A dish from the Parsi community of Bombay, served at all their wedding banquets. Fish is smothered in a fresh coconut chutney, wrapped in banana leaves and steamed. Having no easy access to banana leaves, I have used foil.

In India, pomfret is used for this dish. Instead, you may use thick steaks of bass, pampano or red snapper – or thick chunks of cod, halibut or haddock. Salmon steaks, however extravagant, work quite superbly.

METHOD

Coarsly chop the coriander, green chillies and mint. Put these ingredients with the coconut, garlic, cumin seeds, sugar, lemon juice and salt into the container of a food processor or blender. Blend until you have as fine a paste as possible.

Cut four pieces of foil, each 12 in/ 30.5 cm square. Smother a quarter of the chutney on each fish. Fold two opposite ends of the foil over the fish, one after another. Now do the same with the remaining ends.

Prepare a utensil for steaming. I use a large wok, arranging four criss-cross chopsticks at the bottom. You could set a trivet inside a large pan. Now put the vinegar, oil and curry leaves into the pan. This is the liquid that is going to be used for steaming and it should, of course, stay below the fish packets. Bring the liquid to a boil over a medium-high flame. Arrange the fish packets on top of the chopsticks or trivet. Cover. Turn the heat down to medium low and steam gently for 15 minutes or until the fish is just done.

2 ½ oz/ 60 g/ 1 well-packed cup fresh green coriander (Chinese parsley)

5 fresh hot green chillies

small bundle ½ oz/ ¼ cup/ 15 g fresh mint

enough grated fresh coconut to fill a glass measuring jug to the 12 fl oz/ 1 ½ cup/ 350 ml mark

4 cloves garlic, peeled

1 tsp/ 5 ml ground, cumin seeds

2 tsp/ 10 ml sugar

2 ½ –3 tbs/ 37–45 ml lemon juice

1 tsp/ 5 ml salt

about 1 ½ lb/ 700 g, 4 fish steaks, cut about 1 in/ 2.5 cm thick (see recipe note)

8 fl oz/ 1 cup/ 250 ml distilled white malt vinegar or cider vinegar

1 tbs/ 15 ml vegetable oil

8–10 curry leaves, fresh or dried

Maachher Jhol

FISH IN A BENGALI SAUCE

SERVES 4

1 ¾ lb/ 800 g carp
steaks, red snapper
steaks, or any other
firm, white-fleshed fish
(see recipe note) cut
about 4 cm/ 1 ½ in thick
– large fillets should be
cut into pieces no longer
than 2 in/ 5 cm

½ tsp/ 2.5 ml ground
turmeric

½ tsp/ 2.5 ml salt

¼ pint/ ⅔ cup/ 150 ml
mustard oil or vegetable
oil

1 tbs/ 15 ml ground
coriander seeds

1 tsp/ 5 ml ground cumin
seeds

1 ½ tsp/ 7.5 ml finely
grated, peeled fresh
ginger

1 tsp/ 5 ml ground
turmeric

½ tsp/ 2.5 ml red chilli
powder (cayenne
pepper)

½ tsp/ 2.5 ml salt

¼ tsp nigella seeds
(*kalonji*)

T his is Bengal's 'everyday' fish dish – a staple, along with dishes like the *maacher jhals*, without which no meal seems complete. It is eaten with Plain Rice. You may serve any other vegetables and *dal* of your choice with it as well.

Rui, a carp-like fish is often cooked in this 'sauced' style. I used carp, with bone, cut crosswise into 4-cm/ 1 ½-in thick 'steaks' and it worked very well. Heads can be cooked by those who can handle them. They need to be cut up first. If you cannot find carp, use any firm, white-fleshed fish such as haddock, red snapper, halibut, cod or even swordfish. (In the case of swordfish, I always remove the skin and cube the flesh.) Just make sure the fish pieces are at least 1 in/ 2.5 cm thick. If you can't get 'steaks' you may use cut up fillets.

METHOD

Rub the fish well with the ½ tsp/ 5 ml of turmeric and ½ tsp/ 2.5 ml of salt and set aside for 10–15 minutes.

Heat the oil in a non-stick frying pan over a medium flame. If you are using mustard oil, let it get smokingly hot. Now put in the fish pieces and brown lightly on all sides without cooking them through. Gently lift the fish out of the oil and put it on a plate. Turn off the heat.

Combine the ground coriander seeds, the cumin, ginger, 1 tsp/ 5 ml turmeric, chilli powder (cayenne pepper) and ½ tsp/ 2.5 ml of salt in a small bowl. Add 3 tbs/ 45 ml of water and mix.

Remove all but 5 tbs/ 75 ml of oil from the frying pan. Heat the frying pan over a medium flame.

When hot, put in the nigella seeds. A few seconds later, put in the red chillies. As soon as they darken a bit, put in the bay leaves. When the bay leaves start to darken, put in the onion. Stir and fry the onion, lowering the heat, if necessary, until it is translucent and lightly browned. Add the spice paste. Stir and fry it for about 1 minute. Now put in the fish in a single layer as well as 8 fl oz/ 1 cup/ 250 ml of water. Lay the green chillies over the fish. Simmer over a medium heat for 2 minutes, spooning the sauce over the fish pieces as you do so. Now cover, turn the heat to low and cook the fish for 10–15 minutes or until it is just done.

Note: the whole chillies should be eaten only by those who know what they are doing.

4 whole, dried, hot red chillies

2 bay leaves

4 oz/ 100 g, 1 large onion, peeled and fairly finely chopped

3 whole hot green chillies

VEGETABLES

Bharat
___

SMOKED AUBERGINE/ EGGPLANT WITH YOGHURT

SERVES 4–6
___

2 spring onions
(scallions)
___

about 14 oz/ 400 g,
1 medium-sized
aubergine (eggplant)
___

8 fl oz/ 1 cup/ 250 ml
plain yoghurt
___

3 tbs/ 45 ml finely
chopped fresh green
coriander (Chinese
parsley)
___

½ tsp/ 2.25 ml ground,
roasted cumin (p. 148)
___

½ tsp/ 2.5 ml salt
___

freshly ground black
pepper
___

1 tbs/ 15 ml very hot
ghee (clarified butter –
p. 151)
___

T here are many ways to smoke foods. The Muslim Bohris of Gujarat often cook a dish, then set an onion skin 'cup' in the middle of it. Into this 'cup' they put some *ghee* (clarified butter) and then a hot, live piece of charcoal. They cover the dish immediately, allowing the ensuing smoke to perfume the cooked food. Instead of the coal, you could use a broken piece of ceramic tile or a small spoon, well-heated over a flame.

This dish may be served with all Indian meals. It also makes a good dip for raw vegetables and cocktail crisps and crackers.

If you plan to use the charcoal, arrange to have it glowing and handy sometime before you eat.

METHOD

Cut the spring onions (scallions) crosswise into paper-thin rounds all the way up their green sections. Leave to soak in cold water for 30 minutes. Drain and pat dry.

Roast the aubergine (eggplant) over a low naked flame, turning it whenever necessary, until the skin is completely charred and the vegetable is soft. You could, if you prefer, do the same thing under your grill (broiler).

Peel the aubergine (eggplant) under running water, making sure you remove all the charred bits. Cut off the stem end and mash the vegetable. Put in a serving dish. Add the spring onions (scallions).

Beat the yoghurt lightly with a fork or a whisk until it is smooth and creamy. Add it to the dish with the aubergine (eggplant). Also put in the green coriander (Chinese parsley), roasted cumin, salt and black pepper. Mix well.

Now put a very small bowl or a cup-shaped piece of onion skin in the centre of the aubergine-yoghurt mixture. Pour the hot *ghee* into it. Put a small glowing piece of charcoal into the *ghee* and cover the serving dish immediately. Open it after 5 minutes.

This *bharat* may be served at room temperature or cold.

Baigan Ki Kalonji

STIR-FRIED AUBERGINE/ EGGPLANT

SERVES 4

5 tbs/ 75 ml mustard oil
or vegetable oil

1 tsp/ 5 ml *panchphoran*
(p. 154)

⅛ tsp ground asafetida
(optional)

1 lb 2 oz/ 500 g,
1 medium-sized
aubergine (eggplant),
cut, with skin, into 1-in/
2.5-cm cubes

2 tsp/ 10 ml ground
coriander seeds

about ¼ tsp red chilli
powder (cayenne
pepper)

¼ tsp ground turmeric

½ tsp/ 2.5 ml salt

½ tsp/ 2.5 ml ground
amchoor (p. 143) or
about 1 tsp/ 5 ml lemon
juice

lthough this recipe comes from a *maharaj* – professional Brahmin cook – working for a Benares family, the seasonings in it have very Bengali overtones. It is interesting to speculate on the reasons. First of all, Bengal is not very far from Benares – and its influence extends well beyond its borders. Secondly, *maharajs* work for a successful business community of *Banias* and *Marwaris* that have settled over much of the northern half of India. Many live in Calcutta, Bengal's capital, and this could account for some of the cook's leanings.

This dish should be made, ideally, in a heavy wok or *karhai*, though I have cooked it, quite successfully, in a frying pan as well. You could serve it with Chicken with Apricots and Potato Straws, Plain Rice and Tomato and Onion with Yoghurt.

METHOD

Heat the oil in wok, *karhai* or frying pan over a medium-high flame. If you are using mustard oil, let it get very hot and smoke for a few seconds to release its pungency. However, if you are using a different type of oil do not let it get smokingly hot. Put in the *panchphoran* and asafetida. A second or two later, put in the aubergine (eggplant). Stir for 1 minute and turn the heat down to medium. Put in the coriander, chilli powder (cayenne pepper), turmeric and salt. Now keep stirring and frying for 15–20 minutes, adding 1 tbs/ 15 ml of water every minute or so, until the vegetable is cooked. It will brown during this period. Sprinkle the *amchoor* over the top and stir again.

Gaajar Aur Sooay Ki Bhaji

CARROTS WITH DILL

This quick and easy dish from Lucknow in Uttar Pradesh may be served both with Indian and Western meals. It goes particularly well with Skewered Lamb Kebabs made with Cooked Meat or Quick Kebabs and Flaky Pan Bread.

METHOD

Cut the carrots, crosswise, in ⅛-in/ 0.25-cm thick slices.

Cut the ginger, crosswise, into very thin slices. Stacking the slices over each other, cut them, first into very thin strips and then cut the strips into minute dice.

Heat the oil in a frying pan, wok or *karhai* over a medium flame. When hot, put in the cumin seeds. A few seconds later, put in the asafetida. A second later, put in the ginger and green chillies. When the ginger starts to brown, put in the carrots, coriander and turmeric. Stir for 2 minutes. Add the dill and the salt. Stir. Cover, lower the heat and simmer for 1–2 minutes or until the carrots are just done. Lift the carrots out of the pan with a slotted spoon, leaving as much oil behind as possible.

SERVES 4

1 lb/ 450 g carrots, peeled

¼-in/ 0.5-cm cube ginger, peeled

4 tbs/ 60 ml vegetable oil

½ tsp/ 2.5 ml whole cumin seeds

⅛ tsp ground asafetida (optional)

1–2 fresh hot, green chillies, finely chopped

1 tsp/ 5 ml ground coriander seeds

¼ tsp ground turmeric

1 oz/ ⅔ cup/ 25 g cleaned and chopped fresh dill

½ tsp/ 2.5 ml salt

Poriyal

CAULIFLOWER WITH DRIED CHILLIES AND MUSTARD SEEDS

SERVES 4–6

1 ½ lb/ 700 g, 1 head of cauliflower, yielding about ¾ lb/ 350 g of flowerets

5 tbs/ 75 ml vegetable oil

¼ tsp ground asafetida

1 tsp/ 5 ml whole black mustard seeds

1 tsp/ 5 ml skinned *urad dal* (p. 150)

2 whole dried hot red chillies

6 hot, whole fresh green chillies

¾ tbs/ 30 ml grated fresh coconut (optional – p. 145)

This stir-fried dish cooks in 10 minutes and is amazingly good. It has a lot of whole chillies in it, but is not at all hot. The chillies, because they are unbroken, do not give out their heat, lending only the delicate flavour of their red and green skins.

You could serve this cauliflower dish with almost any Indian meal.

METHOD

Cut the cauliflower into small, delicate flowerets. No flowerets should be longer or wider than 1 ½ in/ 4 cm. Longer stems of flowerets may be cut, crosswise, into rounds.

Heat the oil in a wok, *karhai* or frying pan over a medium-high flame. When hot, put in the asafetida. A second later, put in the black mustard seeds. As soon as the mustard seeds begin to pop (this takes just a few seconds), put in the *urad dal*. As soon as the *dal* turns reddish, put in the red and green chillies. When the red chillies start to darken, put in the cauliflower. Stir for 1 minute. Now add the salt and 1 tbs/ 15 ml of water. Stir and cook for 1 minute. Add another 1 tbs/ 15 ml of water if it looks dry. Keep doing this for the next 4 minutes, adding in all about 6 tbs/ ½ cup/ 90 ml of water. Cover, turn the heat to low and cook for about 5 minutes or until the cauliflower is just tender. Remove the lid and dry off any liquid. Add the coconut, if you wish, and stir.

Note: the whole chillies should only be eaten by those who know what they are doing.

Fulvar, Ola Watana Ana Batatya
Chi Bhaji

CAULIFLOWER, PEAS AND POTATOES

This is a mild, soul-satisfying everyday dish, served in nearly all Maharashtrian homes. As it cooks very quickly – in about 15 minutes – most working people find it no trouble at all to put together. Even though I have made the sugar optional, the Maharashtrians almost always use it.

You could serve it with all Indian meals – I find that it is not at all out of place with simple Western meals of grilled (broiled) or roasted meats.

METHOD

Cut the cauliflower into small flowerets – no larger or wider than 1 ½ in/ 4 cm.

If the potatoes are new or the American, small red variety, do not bother to peel them. Cut them into ¾-in/ 2-cm dice or a bit smaller.

Warm the oil in a good-sized frying pan over a medium-high flame. When hot, put in first the asafetida, then, a second later, the mustard seeds. When the mustard seeds begin to pop – this takes just a few seconds, put in the curry leaves. Stir once. Now put in the potatoes, cauliflower, peas, green chillies, turmeric, salt and sugar. Stir for 2 minutes. Add about 2 fl oz/ 50 ml/ ¼ cup of water and stir. As soon as the water begins to bubble, cover and turn the heat to low. Cook for 10–15 minutes or until the potatoes are just done. Sprinkle the coconut and coriander (Chinese parsley) over the top and stir.

SERVES 4–6

12 oz/ 2 cups/ 350 g, when cut, cauliflower (about half a medium-sized head)

8 ½ oz/ 230 g, 3 smallish potatoes, preferably new or red

4 tbs/ ⅓ cup/ 60 ml vegetable oil

⅛ tsp ground asafetida

1 tbs/ 15 ml whole black mustard seeds

8–10 curry leaves, fresh or dried

4 ½ oz/ 1 cup/ 125 g shelled peas, fresh or frozen (if frozen, thaw enough to separate)

2 fresh, hot, green chillies, very finely chopped

¼ tsp ground turmeric

¾ tsp/ 4 ml salt

½ tsp/ 2.5 ml sugar

2 tbs/ 30 ml grated fresh coconut

2 tbs/ 30 ml chopped fresh green coriander (Chinese parsley)

Sookhi Gobi

DRY CAULIFLOWER

SERVES 6

2-in/ 5-cm cube fresh ginger, peeled

6 tbs/ ½ cup/ 90 ml vegetable oil

⅛ tsp ground asafetida

⅛ tsp whole cumin seeds

¼ – ½ tsp red chilli powder (cayenne pepper)

4 tsp/ 20 ml ground coriander seeds

1 tsp/ 5 ml ground turmeric

2 lb/ 900 g head of cauliflower, cut into 1-in/ 2.5-cm flowerets (see above)

1 ½ tsp/ 7 ½ ml salt

½ tsp/ 2.5 ml *garam masala* (p. 151)

1 tsp/ 5 ml ground *amchoor* (p. 143) or 2 tsp/ 10 ml lemon juice (more may be added, if desired)

I t is important for many of India's cauliflower dishes that the vegetable be cut quite small while preserving the shape of the flowerets. To do this, break off a large floweret. Now try breaking or cutting it into small flowerets no wider or longer than 1 in/ 2.5 cm. Long stems should be cut crosswise into ¼-in/ 0.5-cm slices and added to the dish.

METHOD

Cut the ginger, crosswise, into very thin slices. Stacking several of the slices over each other at a time, cut them first into very thin strips and then cut the strips crosswise into minute dice.

Heat the oil in a very large frying pan, wok, *karhai* or other wide utensil over a medium-high flame. When hot, put in the asafetida and, a second later, the cumin seeds. As soon as the cumin seeds begin to sizzle, put in the ginger. Stir the ginger around for a few seconds until it just starts to brown. Now put in the red chilli powder (cayenne pepper), coriander and turmeric. Stir once and quickly put in the cut cauliflower and salt. Stir the cauliflower around for 1 minute. Add 4 tbs/ 60 ml of water and cover the pan immediately. Turn heat to low and cook for 5-10 minutes or until the cauliflower is just done. Stir once or twice during this period. (Add 1 tbs/ 15 ml more water if it seems to dry out.)

When the cauliflower is just done, remove the lid. If there is any liquid in the pan, dry it off by turning up the heat a bit. Sprinkle the *garam masala* and *amchoor* over the top and stir to mix.

Makai Nu Shaak

CORN COOKED WITH MILK

SERVES 4

ere is a dish from the western region of Saurashtra. Maize is generally used, but sweetcorn, available more easily in the West, works quite well. I have even used frozen corn quite satisfactorily.

This is a nice dish to serve at a brunch (with toast) or you could also serve it as a vegetable with any Indian meal.

Use a frying pan or a heavy pan that is good for boiling milk.

10 oz/ 2 ½ cups/ 275 g corn, either taken off a cob or frozen corn that has been dropped in boiling water, defrosted and drained

¾ pint/ 2 cups/ 450 ml whole milk

1 tbs/ 15 ml vegetable oil

⅛ tsp whole cumin seeds

½ tsp/ 2.5 ml very finely grated fresh ginger

1 fresh hot green chilli, very finely chopped

¼ tsp sugar

¼ tsp salt

pinch red chilli powder (cayenne pepper)

2 tbs/ 30 ml freshly grated coconut (p. 145)

1 tbs/ 15 ml finely chopped fresh green coriander (Chinese parsley)

METHOD

Put the corn and the milk in a heavy pan. Bring to a simmer, making sure it does not boil over. Keep simmering vigorously, stirring now and then, until there is very little milk left – just enough to keep the corn looking wet – 2 tbs/ 30 ml.

Heat the oil in a non-stick frying pan or pan over a medium flame. When hot, put in the cumin seeds. A few seconds later, put in the ginger and green chilli. Stir once. Now put in the corn, sugar, salt and red chilli powder (cayenne pepper). Stir to mix. Add the coconut and green coriander (Chinese parsley). Stir to mix again and turn off the heat.

Payaru Thoran

GREEN BEANS WITH COCONUT

1 lb/ 450 g green beans

1 oz/ 25 g, 1 good-sized
shallot, peeled and very
coarsely chopped

1–2 fresh, hot green
chillies, cut into 2–3
pieces each

2 cloves garlic, peeled

3 oz/ 1 cup/ 75 g grated
fresh coconut

1 tsp/ 5 ml ground cumin
seeds

¼ tsp ground turmeric

5 tbs/ 75 ml vegetable
oil

1 tsp/ 5 ml whole
mustard seeds

2 tsp/ 10 ml uncooked
white rice

10–12 fresh or dried
curry leaves

1 whole, dried, hot, red
chilli

about 1 tsp/ 5 ml salt

T here is a very slim, rounded, long bean – almost 1 ft/ 30 cm long – that is available in many Indian and Oriental grocery stores. It is sometimes known as the asparagus bean, or as *lobhia* or, in Malayalam, the language in Kerala, as *payaru*. If you can find it, do use it in this Kerala-style dish. It has a delicate but fairly assertive flavour that is quite delicious (I love eating it raw as well.) On the other hand, almost any green beans may be used – French beans, flat green beans and the more common rounded green beans. If the beans are on the tougher side, it might be a good idea to parboil them quickly first by cutting them, and dropping them into boiling water for 1 minute or so and then draining them.

Thorans may be made with shredded cabbage, spinach, even carrots and peas, if you like. Whatever vegetable you use, cut it into small pieces or shreds so it cooks quickly.

In this dish, raw rice is used very interestingly as a spice. You may serve this versatile *thoran* with almost any Indian meal.

METHOD

Lay several beans down together, trim their ends and then cut them, crosswise, into ¼-in/ 0.5-cm rounds. Do all the beans this way. Put the shallots, green chillies, garlic, coconut, cumin and turmeric into the container of a food processor or blender. Grind to a coarse consistency. Decant into a bowl.

Heat the oil in a large frying pan or wok over a medium-high flame. When hot, put in the mustard seeds and rice. When the mustard seeds begin to pop and the rice swells and turns golden (this just takes a few seconds), put in the curry leaves and the red chilli. When the chilli swells and darkens (this also takes just a few seconds) put in the green beans. Stir and fry them for 2–3 minutes. Now make a hole in the centre of the mound of beans and put the coarsely ground spices there. Cover up the spices with the beans and sprinkle salt evenly over the top. Add 2 tbs/ 30 ml of water to the pan and cover immediately. Turn the heat to low and cook for 10 minutes or until the beans are tender. Mix well and serve.

This *thoran* may be made a couple of hours ahead of time and reheated.

Farasvi Bhaji

GREEN BEANS COOKED WITH SPLIT PEAS

SERVES 4
---

2 tsp/ 10 ml skinned
urad dal or *moong dal*
or yellow split peas
(p. 149)
---

10 oz/ 275 g green
beans
---

3 tbs/ 45 ml vegetable
oil

⅛ tsp ground asafetida
(optional)

½ tsp/ 2.5 ml whole
black mustard seeds

¼ tsp whole cumin
seeds

8–10 curry leaves, fresh
or dried (p. 149)
---

1 whole hot green chilli,
very finely chopped
---

about ½ tsp/ 2.5 ml salt
---

about ½ tsp/ 2.5 ml
sugar

⅛ tsp ground turmeric

¼ tsp ground cumin
seeds
---

1 tsp/ 5 ml ground
coriander seeds

T his delicious bean dish from the Chittapavan
Brahmins of Maharashtra uses an unusual
cooking technique. It can only be described as a
reversed double-boiler method – the food is in
the bottom pot and water on top – with the result
that the food cooks in the minimal water that drips
down as condensation. This is simple to do and is
exceedingly nutritious as all the properties of the
vegetables are conserved. I find myself cooking all
my vegetables this way now. If you have a double-
boiler, do use it. Otherwise, find a second pot that
can sit on the first one, nesting inside it slightly, or
a lid that can hold water on top of it.

You will notice that *dal* (or split peas) has been
added to provide protein. This bean dish may be
served with almost any Indian meal.

METHOD

Pick over the *dal* or yellow split peas and wash.
Drain and put in a small bowl. Add enough water
so it covers the *dal* or split peas by about 1 in/ 2.5
cm. Let the *dal* soak for 30 minutes and the split
peas for 1 hour. Drain.

Trim the ends of the beans and cut crosswise
into ¼-in/ 0.5-cm rounds. Put some water to boil.

Heat the oil in a heavy pan over a medium
heat. When hot, put in first the asafetida, then, a
second later, the mustard seeds and whole cumin
seeds. When the mustard seeds begin to pop (this
just takes a few seconds) put in the curry leaves. Stir
once and put in the drained *dal* or split peas. Stir
a few times until the *dal* is very lightly browned.
Now put in the green beans, the green chillies,

salt, sugar, turmeric, ground cumin and ground coriander. Stir for 1 minute. Turn the heat to low. Put a second pan on top of the first pan and half fill it with boiling water. (If you are using a lid to hold water, just pour as much as it will hold and replenish it now and then.)

Cook for about 10 minutes or until the beans are just done. Remove the pan with the water. Add coconut and fresh green coriander (Chinese parsley). Stir to mix.

2 oz/ ½ cup/ 50 g freshly ground coconut

2 tbs/ 30 ml finely chopped fresh green coriander (Chinese parsley)

Moinja Haak

KOHLRABI GREENS

SERVES 4

1 ¼ lb/ 550 g kohlrabi leaves

5 tbs/ 75 ml mustard oil or olive oil (see recipe note)

½ tsp/ 2.5 ml bicarbonate of soda (baking soda) (optional)

½ tsp/ 2.5 ml salt

2 hot, dried red chillies, deseeded

4–6 cloves garlic, peeled and very coarsely chopped

Kohlrabi, also called knol-kohl, is eaten in its entirety in Kashmir – the leaves as well as the turnip-like ball to which they are attached. This dish calls for just the greens. (The ball may be peeled, sliced, and put into a salad or else sprinkled lightly with salt and pepper – red chilli powder (cayenne pepper) too, if you like – and served with drinks.) If the kohlrabi is picked when the leaves are still tender, the leaves should be used whole, with just their coarse stems broken off. I rarely find such kohlrabi in Western markets. I find that I have to cut up the maturer leaves that are more readily available.

This particular dish may also be made with spring greens in Britain and with collard greens in the United States.

Kashmiris use bicarbonate of soda when cooking leafy vegetables in order to keep them green. You may do so if you are particular about the colour of the dish or else leave it out.

This versatile dish may be served with any Kashmiri meat and Plain Rice or with any North Indian meal. I find that it also tastes particularly good with grilled (broiled) pork chops!

If this dish is to have an authentic Kashmiri taste, it should be cooked with mustard oil. You could, however, substitute olive oil for a different but equally interesting flavour. Do not let the olive oil heat to smoking point.

At a typical Kashmiri meal it would be served with Plain Rice and Lamb with Kashmiri Red Chillies.

METHOD

Wash the kohlrabi leaves and cut away the very coarse stems. If the leaves are large, hold several of them together and cut them crosswise at 2-in/ 5-cm intervals.

Heat the oil in a very large pan over a medium-high flame. Let it get smokingly hot. Let it smoke for a few seconds. (This burns away its pungency and makes it sweet.) Now put in 4 pints/ 10 cups/ 2.25 litres of water, the kohlrabi leaves, the bicarbonate of soda, salt, red chillies and garlic. Bring to a boil. Cook, uncovered, over a medium-high flame for about 1 hour, stirring now and then, until there is just a little liquid left in the pan, about 4 fl oz/ ½ cup/ 125 ml, and the leaves are tender.

Batate Ambat

POTATOES WITH TOMATOES

SERVES 6

1 lb 2 oz/ 500 g new potatoes, or any other firm, waxy potatoes

10 oz/ 275 g, 3 medium-sized tomatoes

4 tbs/ 60 ml vegetable oil

⅛ tsp ground asafetida (optional)

1 tsp/ 5 ml whole black mustard seeds

½ tsp/ 2.5 ml ground turmeric

⅛ – ½ tsp red chilli powder (cayenne pepper)

2 tsp/ 10 ml tamarind paste (p. 155) or lemon juice

1 tsp/ 5 ml salt

2 oz/ ½ cup/ 50 g freshly grated coconut (p. 145)

Cooked by the Sarasvat Brahmins of Maharashtra, this potato dish is flavoured with tomatoes and fresh coconut. Serve it hot with Indian meals or cold as a deliciously spicy potato salad.

METHOD

Cut the potatoes lengthwise (with skin, if using new potatoes) in to 1-in/ 2.5-cm thick fingers. Chop the tomatoes very finely.

Heat the oil in a frying pan or wide pan over a medium-high flame. When hot, put in first the ground asafetida and, a second later, the mustard seeds. As soon as the mustard seeds begin to pop take the pan off the fire and quickly put in the turmeric, red chilli powder (cayenne pepper) and the tomatoes. Cover and put the pan back on the heat for 1 minute. Uncover. Put in about 8 fl oz/ 1 cup/ 250 ml of water, the potatoes, the tamarind paste and salt. Bring to a boil. Cover, lower the heat and simmer gently for 30 minutes or until the potatoes are tender. Add the coconut and continue cooking for 2–3 minutes. Increase the heat a bit during this period if the sauce seems too thin and watery. You should end up with a very thick sauce that clings to the potatoes somewhat.

Batata Nu Shaak

DICED POTATOES WITH TURMERIC AND CUMIN

T his exceedingly simple dish takes just about 15 minutes to cook and is adored by everyone in our household. It may be served with most Indian meals – at picnics, it goes particularly well with breads, pickles and relishes – and it can also be served with Western meals of roasted and grilled (broiled) meats.

It is best to use unskinned new potatoes for this dish. They would, of course, be scrubbed and wiped dry first. I find that if I cut the potatoes ahead of time and leave them soaking in water, the dish, for some reason, does not turn out as well. So cut the potatoes just before you are ready to cook them. If you have a wok, do use it. It is the ideal utensil for this dish. Otherwise, a frying pan will do.

METHOD

Cut the clean potatoes into ½-in/ 1-cm dice. Heat the oil in a wok or frying pan over a medium heat. When hot, put in, in quick succession, first the asafetida and, a second later, the mustard seeds and then the cumin seeds. Now put in the potatoes and stir once or twice. Sprinkle in the turmeric. Continue to stir every now and then and cook for about 15 minutes or until the potatoes are lightly browned and almost done. Sprinkle in the ground coriander, ground cumin, red chilli powder (cayenne pepper) and salt. Stir and cook for another 1–2 minutes.

SERVES 6

1 ½ lb/ 700 g new potatoes (in US, red potatoes work very well), scrubbed but not peeled

5 tbs/ 75 g vegetable oil

⅛ tsp ground asafetida (optional)

½ tsp/ 2.5 ml whole black mustard seeds

½ tsp/ 2.5 ml *whole* cumin seeds

⅛ tsp ground turmeric

½ tsp/ 2.5 ml ground coriander seeds

½ tsp/ 2.5 ml ground cumin seeds

¼ tsp red chilli powder (cayenne pepper)

¾ tsp/ 4 ml salt

Aloo Matar Ki Karhi

POTATOES AND PEAS IN A YOGHURT SAUCE

SERVES 4

1-in/ 2.5-cm fresh ginger, peeled

3 tbs/ 45 ml vegetable oil

½ tsp/ 2.5 ml whole black mustard seeds

½ tsp/ 2.5 ml whole cumin seeds

1–2 fresh, hot, green chillies, very finely chopped

12 oz/ 350 g, 3 medium-sized potatoes, peeled and cut into 1-in/ 2.5-cm dice

⅛ tsp ground turmeric

½ pint/ 1 ¼ cups/ 300 ml plain yoghurt

1 oz/ 25 g/ 2 tablespoons + 1 teaspoon chickpea flour (gram flour/ *besan*)

1 tsp/ 5 ml salt

¼ tsp sugar

5 oz/ 1 cup/ 150 g fresh or frozen, shelled peas (if frozen, defrost enough to separate)

Throughout India, yoghurt is eaten in many forms, including those that require that it be heated. As yoghurt curdles when boiled, it is first stabilized with chickpea flour. The pulse (legume) flour adds extra nutrition to the dish – a very important consideration for India's numerous vegetarians. This recipe comes from one such Benares family of *Banias* or businessmen. *Karhis*, eaten all over India, have endless regional variations and may be served with Plain Rice or with Indian breads. Other meats and vegetables can also be served at the same meal.

METHOD

Cut the ginger, crosswise, into very thin slices. Stacking a few of the slices on top of each other at a time, cut them first into very thin strips and then cut the strips crosswise into minute dice.

Heat the oil in a wide, heavy-based pan over a medium-high flame. When hot, put in the mustard seeds. As soon as the seeds begin to pop (this takes just a few seconds), put in the cumin seeds. A few seconds later, put in the ginger and the green chillies. Stir for ½ minute and put in the potatoes and the turmeric. Stir the potatoes once or twice to mix, and then put in ¼ pint/ ⅔ cup/ 150 ml of water. Cover, turn the heat to low and simmer gently for 6–8 minutes or until the potatoes are just tender.

While the potatoes are cooking, put the yoghurt in a bowl. Beat lightly with a fork or whisk until smooth and creamy. Add ½ pint/ 1 ¼ cups/ 300 ml of water and mix again. Put the chickpea flour in another bowl. Slowly add the yoghurt mixture, mixing all the time to avoid lumps. (If there are any lumps, strain the mixture through a sieve.) Add just ½ tsp/ 2.5 ml of the salt and all the sugar to the yoghurt-chickpea flour mixture and stir.

When the potatoes are just tender, add the peas and the remaining ½ tsp/ 2.5 ml of salt. Mix. Cover and continue to cook for 2–3 minutes or until the peas are tender. Now pour in the yoghurt-chickpea flour mixture. Stir as you bring it to a simmer over a medium flame. Lower the flame again and simmer gently for 2 minutes.

Aloo Bhaji

SPICY POTATOES

SERVES 4

1 ½ lb / 700 g, 5 medium-sized firm, waxy potatoes, preferably new or red

¾-in/ 2-cm cube fresh ginger, peeled

5 tbs/ 75 ml vegetable oil

1 tsp/ 5 ml whole black mustard seeds

½ tsp/ 2.5 ml whole cumin seeds

pinch ground asafetida

1–2 fresh, hot green chillies, very finely chopped

1 ½ tsp/ 7.5 ml ground coriander seeds

¼ tsp ground turmeric

½ tsp/ 2.5 ml red chilli (cayenne pepper)

1–1 ½ tsp/ 5–7.5 ml ground *amchoor* (p. 143) or lemon juice

1–1 ½ tsp/ 5–75 ml salt

¾ tsp/ 4 ml *garam masala* (p. 151)

I had this exquisite potato dish for breakfast in the bazaars of the old city of Benares, where it was served with *kachoris*, stuffed fried breads, and pickles. The potatoes are never cut with a knife. They are just boiled and peeled and then broken by hand into small pieces. They are best eaten with Pooris.

METHOD

Boil the potatoes. Allow them to cool a bit and peel. Break them by hand so that no piece is larger than ½ in/ 1 cm on any of its sides. There will be some very small pieces but that is as it should be.

Cut the ginger crosswise into very thin slices. Stacking several slices over each other, cut them first into very thin strips and then cut the strips, crosswise, into minute dice.

Heat the oil in a wok, *karhai* or a non-stick frying pan over a medium flame. When hot, put in the mustard seeds. As soon as the seeds begin to pop, put in first the cumin seeds and, a second later, the asafetida. Now put in the ginger and green chillies. Stir for a few seconds until the ginger gets lightly browned. Now put in the coriander, turmeric and red chilli powder (cayenne pepper). Stir once and put in all the broken potatoes. Stir and fry for 1 minute. Now put in about 4 fl oz/ ½ cup / 125 ml of water. Lower the heat and mix gently for ½ minute. Add the *amchoor*, salt and *garam masala*. Stir gently to mix and cook for another minute.

Sorse Dharush

OKRA WITH MUSTARD SEEDS

SERVES 4

G round mustard seeds are used to make the sauce for this dish. They can be slightly bitter – in fact, that is their charm. If you cannot find black mustard seeds, use 2 tbs/ 30 ml of the common yellow kind.

You may serve this with almost any Indian meal.

1 lb/ 450 g whole, fresh okra

1 tbs/ 15 ml whole black mustard seeds

1 tsp/ 5 ml whole yellow mustard seeds

½ tsp/ 2.5 ml ground turmeric

½ – ¾ tsp/ 2.5–4 ml red chilli powder (cayenne pepper)

1 tsp/ 5 ml salt

3 tbs/ 45 ml vegetable oil

⅛ tsp nigella seed (kalonji)

2 fresh, hot green chillies

METHOD

Wash the okra and pat it dry. Cut off the very tips of the pods. Peel the cone-shaped top.

Put the black and the yellow mustard seeds into the container of a clean coffee grinder or other spice grinder. Grind. Put the ground mustard seeds into a small bowl. Add the turmeric, chilli powder (cayenne pepper), salt and ¼ pint/ ½ cup/ 125 ml + 2 tablespoons of water. Stir to mix.

Heat the oil in a large frying pan over a medium flame. When hot, put in the nigella seeds. Ten seconds later, put in the okra and stir. Stir and fry the okra on a medium-low heat for 10 minutes or until it is lightly browned. Add the spice mixture and the green chillies. Bring to a simmer. Cover, lower the heat and simmer gently for 5–8 minutes or until the okra is tender.

Mooli Ka Saag

RADISHES COOKED WITH THEIR LEAVES

SERVES 4

about 1 ½ lb/ 700 g,
2 large bunches white
radish (*mooli*) or red
radishes with green
leaves

1-in/ 2.5-cm cube fresh
ginger, peeled

3–5 fresh, hot green
chillies

5 tbs/ 75 ml vegetable
oil

about ½ tsp/ 2.5 ml salt

2 tsp/ 10 ml ground
coriander seeds

1 tsp/ 5 ml ground cumin
seeds

¼ tsp ground turmeric

A simple dish, enjoyed equally by peasants and jetsetters in Uttar Pradesh, this may be served with almost all Indian meals. It has a slightly bitter taste that I happen to adore. I love it best with a sauced meat or chicken dish, some plain yoghurt, an Indian bread and some nice, hot pickle.

Normally, long white radishes (*mooli*) are used in India, but you can substitute ordinary radishes.

METHOD

Break off and separate the radish leaves. Wash well to remove all grit. Holding a handful of greens at a time, cut crosswise at ¼-in/ 0.5-cm intervals, chopping up both the leaves and the stems. Put in a bowl.

Wash the radishes and discard their tails. Cut them into ¼-in/ 0.5-cm dice.

Cut the ginger, crosswise, into very fine slices. Stacking several slices over each other at a time, cut them first into very thin strips and then cut the strips, crosswise, into minute dice. Cut the green chillies, crosswise, into very thin slices.

Heat the oil in a large, non-stick frying pan, wok or *karhai* over a medium-high flame. When hot, put in the ginger and the green chillies. Stir and fry until the ginger starts to brown. Now put in the chopped radish leaves, the chopped radishes, salt, coriander, cumin and turmeric. Stir. Cover and cook on a medium-low heat for about 15 minutes or until the greens are tender. Remove the cover, turn the heat up and boil away any liquid that may have formed.

KASHMIRI SPINACH

SERVES 4–6

I do not have a Kashmiri name for this dish as I have substituted ordinary spinach for the very different varieties found in Kashmir. This dish is normally hot and spicy. It is often eaten with plain rice and a mild meat dish. I have frequently served it with a very Delhi-style dish – Moghlai Chicken braised with Almonds and Raisins. The two complement each other rather well. Instead of Kashmiri *ver*, I have used *garam masala*. The bicarbonate of soda helps keep the spinach green, but may be omitted.

5 tbs/ 75 ml mustard or vegetable oil

⅛ tsp ground asafetida

2 ½ lb/ 1.1 kg fresh spinach, washed and chopped

½ tsp/ 2.5 ml ground turmeric

½ tsp/ 2.5 ml red chilli powder (cayenne pepper) – use more or less as desired

about 1 ¼ tsp/ 6 ml salt

½ tsp/ 2.5 ml bicarbonate of soda (baking soda) (optional)

¼ tsp *garam masala* (p. 151)

METHOD

Heat the oil in a very large pan over a high flame. If you are using mustard oil, let it get so hot that it smokes. Let it smoke for a few seconds to burn away its pungency. Now put in the asafetida and then all the spinach. Stir the spinach around. Add the turmeric, chilli powder (cayenne pepper), salt and bicarbonate of soda. Continue to cook and stir until the spinach has wilted. Add ¾ pint/ 475 ml/ 2 cups of water. Cook, uncovered, over a medium-high flame, for about 25 minutes or until just a little liquid is left. Stir a few times during this period. Turn the heat to low and mash the spinach with the back of a spoon. Continue to cook, uncovered, for another 10 minutes. Sprinkle *garam masala* over the top and mix.

Moghlai Saag

MOGHLAI SPINACH

SERVES 6

———

3 lb/ 1.4 kg fresh spinach

———

fresh ginger, about 2 in/
5 cm × 1 in/ 2.5 cm ×
1 in/ 2.5 cm

———

4 tbs/ 60 ml vegetable
oil

———

2 oz/ 50 g/ 4 tbs
unsalted butter

———

½ tsp/ 2.5 ml whole
fennel seeds

———

4 whole cardamom pods

———

10 oz/ 275 g, 3 medium-
sized onions, peeled,
cut in half lengthwise
and then cut crosswise
into fine half rings

———

1 tsp/ 5 ml salt

———

¼ tsp red chilli powder
(cayenne pepper)

———

½ tsp/ 2.5 ml *garam
masala* (p. 151)

———

T his wonderfully simple spinach dish is cooked
according to a sixteenth-century Moghul
recipe. You could serve it with almost any meat
dish and rice or as part of a vegetarian meal.

METHOD

Wash the spinach well and set it aside.

Peel the ginger and cut it into very fine slices.
Stack a few slices together at a time and cut into
fine julienne strips.

Over a medium-high flame, heat the oil and
butter in a pan large enough to hold all the spinach.
When the fat is hot, put in the fennel seeds and cardamom pods. Stir once and add the onions and
ginger. Stir and fry until the onions turn a rich,
brown colour. Now put in all the spinach, stuffing
it into the pan, if necessary. Cover, and allow the
spinach to wilt completely. Stir every now and
then. When the spinach has wilted, turn the heat
to medium, add the salt and chilli powder (cayenne
pepper), cover and cook for 25 minutes.

Remove the lid and add the *garam masala*. Stir
and cook the spinach, uncovered, for another 5
minutes or until there is hardly any liquid left at the
bottom of the pan.

Soppu Pallya

MYSORE SPINACH WITH DILL

This dish comes from the palace in Mysore. It is very elegant – and very delicious. It may be served with both Indian and Western meals. It goes particularly well with Chettinad Fried Chicken, Plain Rice and Mango Salad.

METHOD

Separate the spinach leaves and wash them well. Holding a good handful, cut them, crosswise, at ½ in/ 1 cm intervals.

Put the spinach and dill in a large pan. Cover and cook on a medium-low heat. The spinach will cook in its own juices. Stir once or twice and cook for about 20 minutes or until the spinach is tender. Remove the lid and add the salt and the cream. Turn the heat up a bit and boil away most of the liquid, stirring as you do so. There should be just enough liquid left to keep the spinach moist.

Heat the *ghee* in a small frying pan over a medium flame. When hot, put in the black mustard seeds. As soon as the mustard seeds begin to pop (this just takes a few seconds) put in the cumin seeds.

A few seconds later, put in the red chilli. When the chilli starts to darken, empty the contents of the frying pan into the pan with the spinach. Stir to mix.

SERVES 3–4

1 ½ lb/ 700 g fresh spinach

2 oz/ ½ cup/ 50 g chopped dill

½ – ¾ tsp/ 2.5–4 ml salt

4 tbs/ ⅓ cup/ 60 ml single (heavy) cream

1 tbs/ 15 ml *ghee* (p. 151) or vegetable oil

¼ tsp whole black mustard seeds

⅛ tsp whole cumin seeds

1 whole dried, hot red chilli

Kootu

VEGETABLES COOKED WITH SPLIT PEAS

SERVES 6

3 oz/ ½ cup/ 75 g
skinned *chana dal* or
yellow split peas
(p. 149)

10 oz/ 275 g, 3 smallish
potatoes

¼ tsp ground turmeric

¼ tsp ground red chilli
powder (cayenne
pepper)

about 1 lb/ 450 g, half of
a medium-sized green
cabbage, cored and
shredded

2 fresh, hot green
chillies, cut into very
fine rounds

about ½ tsp/ 2.5 ml salt

4 oz/ 1 cup/ 100 g grated
fresh coconut (p. 145)

1 tsp/ 5 ml ground cumin
seeds

2 tbs/ 30 ml vegetable
oil

½ tsp/ 2.5 ml whole
mustard seeds

½ tsp/ 2.5 ml skinned
urad dal, if available
(p. 150)

A ll kinds of vegetables – pumpkin, carrot, spinach, string beans – are combined with *chana dal* in Kerala to make a very nourishing dish which most of northern India has never heard of – *kootu*. Even the texture of the dish is very Southern – neither wet, like a *dal*, nor dry but something in between so it can be eaten with rice. Yoghurt dishes and Plain Rice are almost always served with it, especially by Kerala's vegetarians. In the following recipe I use potatoes and cabbage.

METHOD

Pick over the *chana dal* and wash it in several changes of water. Drain. Put it in a small, heavy pan. Add 12 fl oz/ 1 ½ cups/ 350 ml/ of water and bring to a boil. Turn heat to low, cover partially and cook for about 1 hour or until the *dal* is tender but not mushy. Make sure that the water does not evaporate entirely. Add 1–2 tbs/ 15–20 ml of hot water if necessary. Set the *dal* aside. Wash the potatoes and peel them if they are old otherwise leave them with their skins on. Dice into ½-in/ 1-cm cubes.

Put the potatoes in a wide pan along with ¾ pint/ 2 cups/ 450 ml of water, the turmeric and chilli powder (cayenne pepper). Bring to a boil. Cover, lower the heat and simmer for 7–8 minutes or until the potatoes are almost tender. Now put in the cooked *dal*, the cabbage, green chillies and salt. Cook, stirring gently over a moderately high heat until the cabbage is just tender and just a little liquid is left in the bottom of the pan.

Put the coconut and cumin seeds in the centre

of the pan and cover with the cabbage and potatoes. Cover with a lid, turn heat to low and steam for 2 minutes.

Heat the oil in a small frying pan. When very hot, put in the mustard seeds, then the *urad dal* and rice. When the *urad dal* reddens and the rice turns golden, put in the red chilli and the curry leaves. As soon as the chilli darkens, empty the contents of the small frying pan into the pan with the vegetables. Gently stir the vegetables.

½ tsp/ 2.5 ml uncooked, white rice

1 hot, dried, red chilli, broken into 2 pieces

10 fresh or dried curry leaves (p. 149)

Sai Bhaji

Puréed Vegetables

SERVES 6–8

6 oz/ ½ cup/ 175 g
skinned *chana dal* or
yellow split peas
(p. 149)

3 tbs/ 45 ml vegetable
oil

1 ¼ lb/ 550 g washed
fresh leaf spinach or 2 ×
10-oz/ 283-g packets of
frozen leaf spinach

6–7 oz/ 175–200 g,
1 large potato, peeled
and diced

3 oz/ 75 g, 1 medium-
sized onion, peeled and
coarsely chopped

1 ¼ lb/ 550 g, 4
medium-sized tomatoes,
chopped

5 fresh, hot, green
chillies

1 tsp/ 5 ml salt

I have had many puréed vegetables – carrots and peas and spinach, even artichoke hearts – some in the finest of French restaurants. None of them has ever been as good as this one from the former Indian state of Sindh (now in Pakistan). It is really a happy medley of vegetables, as it combines spinach, potatoes and tomatoes. Some people like to add sorrel and dill as well. Sindhis eat it with Rice Cooked with Split Peas. I often serve it with either Lamb Cooked in the Kolhapuri Style or with Moghlai Chicken Braised with Almonds and Raisins, and rice.

It can be served with most Western meals as it is very delicately spiced.

METHOD

Wash the *chana dal* well and leave it to soak, covered by about 1 in/ 2.5 cm of water, for 1 hour. Drain.

Heat the oil in a large pan over a medium-high flame. When hot, put in all the ingredients as well as 1 ¼ pints/ 3 cups/ ¾ litre of water and bring to a boil. Cover, turn heat to low and boil for 1 hour. Remove the cover, turn the heat up to high and boil rapidly for another 20 minutes or until the liquid is reduced and what remains looks a bit like a thick stew.

Pour this, in two batches, if necessary, into the container of a blender or food processor. Blend. You should end up with a thick purée.

PULSES AND LEGUMES

SERVES 6

7 oz/ 1 cup/ 200 g
skinned *toovar dal* or
yellow split peas
(p. 149)

⅛ tsp ground turmeric

1 tbs/ 15 ml peeled and
very finely chopped
shallots

1 tsp/ 5 ml ground cumin
seeds

3–4 whole fresh, hot
green chillies, slit down
their middles

4 tbs/ 60 ml vegetable
oil or 2 tbs/ 30 ml
coconut oil and 2 tbs/
30 ml *ghee*

½ tsp/ 2.5 ml whole
black mustard seeds

10–12 fresh or dried
curry leaves

1–2 whole, hot, dried
red chillies broken up
into 2–4 pieces each

2 tbs/ 30 ml peeled and
finely sliced shallots

2 cloves garlic, peeled
and finely chopped

5 oz/ 150 g, 1 medium-
sized tomato, chopped

¾–1 tsp/ 4–5 ml salt

½ pint/ 1 ¼ cups/
300 ml, tinned or fresh,
unsweetened coconut
milk (p. 146)

Molaghashyam

DAL CURRY – DAL WITH COCONUT MILK

I n Kerala, *toovar dal*, with its earthy taste and colour is mellowed by the addition of coconut and perked up by curry leaves.

METHOD

Pick over the *dal* and wash it in several changes of water. Drain. Put it in a heavy-based pan and add 1 ½ pints/ 3 ¾ cups/ 900 ml of water as well as the turmeric. Bring to a boil. Turn the heat to low and cover, leaving the lid slightly ajar. Simmer the *dal* for about 45 minutes. Now put in the chopped shallots and ground cumin. Stir, cover in the same way as before and cook for another 15 minutes. Add the green chillies and cook for 10-15 minutes or until the *dal* is tender. If the *dal* seems too thick at any point, add up to 4 fl oz/ ½ cup/ 125 ml of boiling water. The *dal*, at this stage, should be like a thick, paste-like soup. Leave on a very low heat as you complete the final step.

Heat the oil in a small frying pan over a medi-um flame. When hot, put in the mustard seeds. As soon as the mustard seeds begin to pop, (this takes just a few seconds), put in the curry leaves and the red chillies. When the red chillies darken (this happens almost immediately), put in all the sliced shallots and garlic. Stir and fry until the shallots turn a reddish-brown colour. Now add the toma-to pieces. Stir and fry until they soften.

Pour the entire contents of the small frying pan into the *dal*. Add the salt and mix. Add the coconut milk and stir it in.

The *dal* may be cooked several hours ahead of time and then reheated.

Bhaja Moong Dal

ROASTED MOONG DAL WITH SPINACH

SERVES 4–6

his earthy dish has a delightful flavour which comes from roasting the grains of *dal* before cooking them in water. In Bengal, it is generally served with rice and a fried vegetable.

METHOD

Pick over the *dal*. Put it on a clean tea towel (dish towel). Rub it gently to remove as much surface dust as possible. Heat a cast-iron frying pan over a medium-low flame. Allow it to get hot and then put the *dal* in it. Stir and roast until many of the grains turn golden-red. (The colour will not be uniform, but that is all right.) Put the roasted *dal* in a bowl and wash it in several changes of water. Drain.

Put the *dal* in a heavy-based pan. Add the turmeric, bay leaf and 1 ½ pints/ 4 cups/ 900 ml of water. Stir and bring to a simmer. Turn the heat to low, cover, leaving the lid slightly ajar, and cook gently for about 1 hour until the grains are quite tender.

Add the spinach, salt, red chilli powder (cayenne pepper) and ¼ pint/ ⅔ cup /125 ml of water. Stir and bring to a simmer. Cover and simmer gently for 30 minutes, stirring once or twice during this cooking period.

Heat the *ghee* in a small pan or frying pan. When hot, put in the *panchphoran*. A few seconds later, when the seeds start to pop and sizzle, put in the red or green chillies. Stir once and then pour the contents of the small pan or frying pan over the cooked *dal*. Cover immediately.

Note: the whole chillies should only be eaten by those who know what they are doing.

6 ½ oz/ 1 cup/ 190 g skinned *moong dal* (p. 149)

½ tsp/ 2.5 ml ground turmeric

1 bay leaf

¾ lb/ 350 g spinach, washed and cut into ½-in/ 2.5-cm wide shreds

1 tsp/ about 5 ml salt

½ tsp/ 2.5 ml red chilli powder (cayenne pepper)

1 tbs/ 15 ml *ghee* or vegetable oil

½ tsp/ 2.5 ml *panchphoran* (p. 154) or cumin seeds

2 fresh, hot red or green chillies, cut into 1-in/ 2.5-cm pieces

Mili Hui Moong Aur Masoor Dal

MOONG DAL COOKED WITH RED SPLIT LENTILS

SERVES 4

3 oz/ ½ cup/ 75 g
skinned *moong dal*
(p. 149)

2 ½ oz/ ½ cup/ 65 g
skinned, red split lentils
– *masoor dal* – (p. 149)

½ tsp/ 2.5 ml ground
turmeric

¾ tsp/ 4 ml salt

3 tbs/ 45 ml vegetable
oil

a small pinch of ground
asafetida (optional)

½ tsp/ 2.5 ml whole
cumin seeds

2 cloves garlic, peeled
and finely chopped

1 oz/ 25 g, 1 small onion,
peeled, cut in half
lengthwise and then
cut finely crosswise

3 oz/ 75 g, 1 small
tomato, chopped

½ tsp/ 2.5 ml ground
coriander seeds

½ tsp/ 2.5 ml ground
cumin seeds

¼ tsp red chilli powder
(cayenne pepper)

I n my family, we eat this simple, earthy dish quite frequently, generally with plain Basmati rice, a vegetable, such as spinach and, if we are feeling like meat, then Moghlai Chicken braised with Almonds and Raisins goes well with it.

METHOD

Pick over the *moong dal* and the red split lentils. Put them in a bowl and wash them in several changes of water. Drain and put in a small, heavy pan with 1 ½ pints/ 4 cups/ 900 ml of water and the turmeric. Bring to a boil. Cover partially, turn the heat to low and simmer gently for 1 hour or longer until soft. Add the salt and stir it in.

Heat the oil in a small frying pan over a medium flame. When hot, put in the asafetida. A few seconds later, put in the whole cumin seeds. A few seconds after that, put in the garlic and onion. Stir and fry until the onion is browned. Now put in the tomato. Stir and cook until the tomato is soft. Put in the ground coriander, ground cumin and red chilli powder (cayenne pepper). Stir once and add the contents of the frying pan to the cooked *dal*. Stir to mix. This *dal* can be reheated easily over a lowish flame.

Razma Gogji

RED KIDNEY BEANS COOKED WITH TURNIPS

his Kashmiri dish is perfect for cold days. It may be served with Plain Rice and any lamb or chicken dish. I sometimes eat it all by itself with some crusty wholemeal bread and a green salad!

METHOD

Put the red kidney beans in a large pan. Add 2 pints/ 5 cups/ 1.1 litres of water and bring to a boil. Boil vigorously for 10 minutes. Turn the heat down and simmer, partially covered, for 1–1½ hours or until cooked through.

Meanwhile, peel the turnips and cut into 4 wedges each.

Put the ground ginger, turmeric, salt and chilli powder (cayenne pepper) into a small bowl. Add 1 tbs/ 15 ml of water and mix to a smooth paste.

Heat the oil in a frying pan over a medium heat. When hot, put in the turnip pieces and brown them on all sides. Remove the turnip pieces with a slotted spoon and set aside. Now put the onion into the same oil. Stir and fry until the onion is a medium brown colour. Turn the heat down slightly and put in the garlic. Stir for a few seconds. Now put in the spice paste from the small bowl. Stir once and turn the heat off.

When the beans have cooked for 45 minutes, add the turnips as well as the onion mixture in the frying pan to the pan of beans. Stir. Ladle a little of the bean liquid into the frying pan, swish it around and pour it back into the bean pan. Bring the beans to a vigorous simmer. Turn heat down to low, cover partially and simmer gently for another 45 minutes or until cooked through.

SERVES 6

5 ½ oz/ 1 cup/ 160 g red kidney beans, picked over and well washed, soaked overnight, drained

14 oz/ 400 g, 4 medium-sized turnips

¼ tsp ground ginger (*sont*)

¼ tsp ground turmeric

1 tsp/ 5 ml salt

⅛–½ tsp red chilli powder (cayenne pepper)

4 tbs/ 60 ml vegetable oil

1 medium-sized onion, peeled, cut in half lengthwise and then cut crosswise into fine half rings

2–3 cloves garlic, peeled and finely chopped

Dalcha

RED SPLIT LENTILS COOKED WITH LAMB

SERVES 6

8 oz/ 1 ½ cups/ 225 g
skinned red split lentils
(*masoor dal* – p. 149)

½ tsp/ 2.5 ml ground
turmeric

4 tbs/ 60 ml vegetable
oil

1 ½-in/ 4-cm cinnamon
stick

6 whole cardamom pods

3 oz/ 75 g, 1 medium-
sized onion, peeled, cut
in half lengthwise and
then cut crosswise into
fine half rings

½ lb/ 225 g boneless
meat from lamb
shoulder, cut into 1-in/
2.5-cm cubes

1 tsp/ 5 ml peeled and
finely grated fresh
ginger

1 tsp/ 5 ml finely crushed
garlic

¼ tsp red chilli powder
(cayenne pepper)

¼–⅓ tsp salt

Not much lamb is used in this Hyderabadi dish – just ½ lb/ 225 g – making it perfect for those who are trying to cut down on their meat intake. You may serve it with rice, some green vegetables and a yoghurt dish.

METHOD

Pick over the lentils and then wash them in several changes of water. Drain. Put them in a heavy-based pan. Add 1 ½ pints/ 3 ¾ cups/ 900 ml of water and the turmeric. Bring to a simmer. Cover, leaving the lid slightly ajar and simmer gently for about 1 ¼ hours or until the lentils are quite tender.

While the lentils are cooking, prepare the meat. Heat the 4 tbs/ 60 ml of oil in a wide-based pan over a medium-high flame. When hot, put in the cinnamon and cardamom. Sir for a few seconds or until the cardamom begins to darken a bit. Put in the onions and stir fry until slightly browned. Now put in the meat. Stir the meat around until it browns a little. Now put in the ginger, garlic, ¼ tsp red chilli powder (cayenne pepper) and the ¼–⅓ tsp of salt. Stir for 1 minute to allow the spices to brown. Now put in about 6 fl oz/ ¾ cup/ 175 ml of water and bring to a simmer. Cover tightly and simmer very gently for 1–1 ¼ hours or until the meat is tender. If the water boils away, just add a tiny bit more.

When the lentils are tender, mash them lightly with the back of a spoon. Add the tamarind, the 1 ½ tsp/ 7.5 ml of salt, and the ½ tsp/ 2.5 ml of red chilli powder (cayenne pepper). Stir to mix and taste for the balance of seasonings. Adjust, if necessary.

When the meat is tender, pour the cooked, seasoned lentils over it. Stir to mix. Bring to a simmer and simmer gently, uncovered, for 1 minute.

Heat the *ghee* in a small frying pan over a medium flame. When hot, put in the whole cumin seeds. A few seconds later, put in the whole red chilli and the curry leaves. Stir. As soon as the chilli darkens a bit, put in the garlic cloves. Stir until the garlic turns a medium-brown in colour. Pour the contents of the frying pan over the lentil-meat combination. (You may do this last step after you have put the *dalcha* into a serving dish. The seasonings scattered over the top serve as a garnish.)

Note: the large whole spices in this dish are not meant to be eaten.

3 tbs/ 45 ml tamarind pulp or about 2 tbs/ 30 ml lemon juice

about 1 ½ tsp/ 7.5 ml salt

½ tsp/ 2.5 ml red chilli powder (cayenne pepper)

2 tbs/ 30 ml *ghee* or vegetable oil

½ tsp/ 2.5 ml whole cumin seeds

1–2 dried whole hot red chillies

8–10 fresh or dried curry leaves

2 cloves of garlic, peeled and cut in half lengthwise

Mysore Sambar

MYSORE SPLIT PEAS WITH WHOLE SHALLOTS

SERVES 6

6 oz/ 1 cup/ 175 g
skinned *toovar dal*
(p. 149)

½ tsp/ 2.5 ml ground
turmeric

3 tbs/ 45 ml vegetable
oil

3 ½–4 oz/ 1 cup/ 90–100 g
small shallots, peeled
(larger ones may be
halved, lengthwise)

4 tbs/ ⅓ cup/ 60 ml
tamarind paste (p. 155)

1 ½ tsp/ 7.5 ml salt

2 tbs/ 30 ml *sambar*
powder (next recipe)

1 tbs/ 15 ml *ghee* or
vegetable oil

½ tsp/ 2.5 ml whole
black mustard seeds

6–10 fresh or dried curry
leaves

S *ambars*, eaten all over the South with many local variations, are soupy dishes, made with *toovar dal*. They are meant to be eaten with Plain Rice and are quite fiery. The only way to lessen their heat is to put fewer red chillies in the spice mixture – or *sambar* powder (see recipe opposite) – with which they are seasoned.

METHOD

Pick over the *toovar dal* and wash it in several changes of water. Drain. Put the *dal* in a heavy-based pan. Put in 1 ¾ pints/ 4 ¼ cups/ 1 litre of water and the turmeric. Bring to a simmer. Cover, leaving the lid slightly ajar, lower the heat and simmer gently for 1½ hours. Stir a few times during the last 30 minutes.

Meanwhile, heat the 3 tbs/ 45 ml of oil in another pan over a medium flame. When hot, put in the shallots. Stir and sauté them until they are lightly browned. Now add ¾ pint/ 2 cups/ 450 ml of water, the tamarind paste, salt and *sambar* powder. Stir and bring to a simmer. Cover, lower the heat and simmer gently for about 10 minutes or until the shallots are tender.

Once the *dal* has finished cooking, add it to the pan with the shallots. Stir to mix and simmer for 5 minutes.

Heat the *ghee* in a small frying pan over a medium flame. When hot, put in the black mustard seeds. As soon as they begin to pop, put in the curry leaves. Stir them once and then empty the contents of the frying pan into the pan with the *sambar*.

MYSORE SAMBAR POWDER

The proportions which I have given make a very hot, traditional *sambar*. If you wish to make a medium-hot *sambar*, put in just 1 ½ tbs/ 22.5 ml of dried whole red chillies. For a mild *sambar*, put in just 7–8 of them.

METHOD

Heat 1 tsp/ 5 ml of the oil in a small, cast-iron frying pan. When hot, put in the coriander seeds, cinnamon, asafetida and fenugreek. Stir until the coriander seeds turn a shade darker and emit a roasted aroma. Empty into a bowl. Put the red chillies into the same frying pan. Stir and roast until they start to darken. Put them into the bowl as well. Now put the remaining 1 tsp/ 5 ml of oil in the pan. Put in the *chana dal*. Stir and fry until it turns reddish. Put it into the bowl. Put the coconut and curry leaves into the frying pan. Stir and roast them until the coconut turns a light brown. Put them into the bowl with the spices and mix.

Let the spices cool. Now put them, in batches, if necessary, into the container of a clean coffee grinder or other spice grinder. Grind. The mixture should remain slightly coarse. Put in a tightly sealed bottle and use as needed.

MAKES ENOUGH TO FILL A 6 FL OZ/ ¾ CUP/ 175 ML JAR

2 tsp/ 10 ml vegetable oil

3 tbs/ 45 ml whole coriander seeds

2 x 1-in/ 2.5-cm cinnamon sticks, broken up

⅓-in/ 0.5-cm cube of solid asafetida (just break off a lump with a hammer)

⅛ tsp whole fenugreek seeds

3 tbs/ 45 ml or less (see recipe note) whole, dried hot red chillies

2 tbs/ 30 ml skinned *chana dal* (p. 149)

4 tbs/ ⅓ cup/ 60 ml dessicated, unsweetened coconut

15–20 fresh or dried curry leaves

Karhi

CHICKPEA FLOUR STEW WITH DUMPLINGS

SERVES 6

¾ pint/ 2 cups/ 450 ml plain yoghurt

4 oz/ 1 cup/ 100 g chickpea flour (gram flour/ *besan*)

2 tbs/ 30 ml vegetable oil

¼ tsp whole cumin seeds

¼ tsp whole fennel seeds

¼ tsp nigella seeds (*kalonji*)

15 fenugreek seeds (*methi*)

1–2 whole, dried, hot, red chillies

¼ tsp ground turmeric

1 tsp/ 5 ml salt

W̲e often had this soupy stew, filled with bobbing dumplings, as part of our Sunday lunch. I still serve it, with plain Basmati rice, Skewered Lamb Kebabs, a vegetable such as spinach or okra, and a crunchy salad such as Tomato, Onion and Cucumber Relish.

METHOD

Put the ¾ pint/ 450 ml/ 2 cups of yoghurt in a large bowl. Beat lightly with a fork or whisk until smooth and creamy. Slowly add 2 pints/ 1.1 litres/ 5 cups of water and mix.

Put 4 oz/ 100 g/ 1 cup of chickpea flour in another large bowl. Very slowly, add the yoghurt mixture, a little at a time, mixing well as you do so. If lumps form, remove them as you go along before adding more of the yogurt mixture. If the final paste is a bit lumpy, just strain it.

Heat the 2 tbs/ 30 ml of oil in a large pan over a medium flame. When hot, put in the whole cumin seeds, fennel seeds, nigella seeds, fenugreek seeds and, last of all, the red chillies. When the chillies darken (this just takes seconds), put in the turmeric and, a moment later, the chickpea flour and yoghurt mixture. Add the salt and bring to a boil. Turn heat to low, cover partially and simmer gently for 25 minutes. Turn off the heat.

While the *karhi* is cooking, make the dumplings. Put the 4 oz/ 1 cup/ 100 g of chickpea flour for the dumplings in a bowl. Add the salt and the bicarbonate of soda. Mix. Add the 4 fl oz/ ½ cup/ 125 ml yoghurt and mix well with a wooden spoon. You should have a thick but 'droppable' paste. If necessary, add another 1 tsp/ 5 ml of yoghurt. Continue to beat the paste vigorously with the wooden spoon for about 10 minutes or until it becomes light and airy.

Pour vegetable oil into a large frying pan to a depth of ¾ in/ 2 cm. Heat the oil over a medium flame. When hot, lift up a blob of paste, about ¾ in/ 2 cm in diameter, on the tip of a teaspoon. Release it into the oil with the help of a second teaspoon. Make all the dumplings this way, dropping them into the oil in quick succession. Turn the dumplings around and fry them slowly until they are reddish in colour and cooked through. Remove the dumplings with a slotted spoon and place on a plate lined with absorbent kitchen paper (paper towels). Let them cool slightly and then cover tightly.

Ten minutes before you sit down to eat, heat the *karhi* over a medium flame. When hot, put in all the dumplings. Cover and continue to simmer over a low flame for another 10 minutes.

For the dumplings

4 oz/ 1 cup/ 100 g chickpea flour (gram flour/ *besan*)

¼ tsp salt

½ tsp/ 2.5 ml bicarbonate of soda (baking soda)

about 4 fl oz/ ½ cup/ 125 ml plain yoghurt

vegetable oil

Punjabi Lobhia

PUNJABI BLACK-EYED BEANS/ BLACK-EYED PEAS

SERVES 6

½ lb/ 1 ½ cups/ 225 g dried black-eyed beans (black-eyed peas) picked over and washed

2 x 1-in/ 2.5-cm cubes of fresh ginger, peeled and coarsely chopped

6–7 cloves garlic, peeled and coarsely chopped

5 tbs/ 75 ml/ 6 tbs vegetable oil or *ghee* (p. 151)

6 ½ oz/ 190 g, 2 medium-sized onions, peeled and finely chopped

2 tsp/ 10 ml ground coriander seeds

1 tsp/ 5 ml ground cumin seeds

4 oz/ 100 g, 1 large tomato, chopped

4 tbs/ ⅓ cup/ 60 ml plain yoghurt

¼–1 tsp red chilli powder (cayenne pepper)

A hearty lunch-time favourite in the Punjab, this is generally served with a bread – such as *parathas*. Yoghurt, another vegetable dish such as cauliflower, meats and relishes may also be served at the same meal.

METHOD

Drain the beans. Put them in a pan with 2 pints/ 5 cups/ 1.1 litres of water and bring to a boil. Cover, lower the heat and simmer gently for 2 minutes. Turn off the flame. Let the pan sit, covered and undisturbed for 1 hour.

Put the ginger and garlic, along with 4 tbs/ ⅓ cup/ 60 ml of water, into the container of a food processor or electric blender. Blend until you have a paste.

Heat the oil in a heavy pan over a medium-high flame. When hot, put in the onions. Stir and fry until the onions are a medium-brown colour. Add the ginger-garlic paste. Stir and fry for 1 minute. Now put in the ground coriander and cumin. Stir for another minute. Put in the tomato. Stir and fry until the tomato is soft. Turn heat to medium. Continue to stir and fry for 2 minutes. Add 1 tbs/ 15 ml of the yoghurt. Stir and fry until the yoghurt is incorporated into the sauce. Add all the yoghurt this way, 1 tbs/ 15 ml at a time, until it is all incorporated. Continue to stir and fry for 2–3 minutes. Now add the beans and their liquid, the red chilli powder (cayenne pepper) and salt. Stir to mix and bring to a simmer. Cover, turn the heat to low and simmer gently for about 40 minutes or until the beans are tender. If there is a lot of liquid, turn up the flame a bit, remove the cover and cook for another 10 minutes or until the liquid is reduced. The beans should look fairly thick.

Sprinkle the fresh green coriander (Chinese parsley) over the top when serving.

1 ¼ tsp/ 6 ml salt

2 tbs/ 30 ml finely chopped fresh green coriander (Chinese parsley)

Dhoklas

STEAMED SAVOURY CAKES

SERVES 6–8

6 ¼ oz/ 1 cup/ 180 g
skinned *chana dal*
(p. 149)

3 oz/ ½ cup/ 75 g
long-grain rice

1 ¼ oz/ 35 g/ ¼ cup
skinned *urad dal* (p. 150)

1 tsp/ 5 ml salt

1 ¼ tsp/ 6 ml peeled and
very finely grated fresh
ginger

1 tsp/ 5 ml very finely
minced fresh green
chillies

¼ tsp whole cumin
seeds

2 fl oz/ ¼ cup/ 50 ml
vegetable oil

¼ tsp bicarbonate of
soda (baking soda)

3 tbs/ 45 ml vegetable
oil

1 tbs/ 15 ml whole black
mustard seeds

2 tbs/ 30 ml whole
sesame seeds

2–3 whole, dried hot red
chillies

S pongy to the touch and covered with mustard and sesame seeds, *dhokla* squares are a savoury and may be served with tea or as part of a meal. Chutneys – such as Yoghurt Chutney and Sesame Seed Chutney – may be used as a dip.

Dhoklas are very simple to make but they do need about 30 hours for soaking and fermentation.

METHOD

Pick over the *chana dal*, rice and *urad dal* and wash together in several changes of water. Drain. Cover with water by 3 in/ 7.5 cm and leave to soak for 8 hours. Drain.

Put the *dal* and rice mixture into the container of a food processor or blender. Blend, pushing down with a rubber spatula whenever necessary. When you have a coarse paste, add 8 fl oz/ 1 cup/ 250 ml of water in a steady, but gentle stream. Continue to blend, again pushing down with a rubber spatula when necessary for a good 6–8 minutes or until you have an airy batter. Empty the batter into a bowl. Cover loosely with an over-turned plate and put in a *warm* place (80°F/ 28°C temperature is ideal) for 20–22 hours or until the batter is *filled* with tiny bubbles. (In very hot climates, this will happen much faster.)

Put the salt, ginger, green chillies and cumin seeds into the bowl with the batter but do *not* stir them in yet.

Get everything ready for steaming. Ideally, you should have two cake tins. They could be 8-in/ 20-cm rounds, with a height of 1-1½ in/ 2.5-4 cm or they could be 8-in/ 20-cm squares of the same height. At a pinch, one cake tin will do. The cake tin should fit easily into some contraption for steaming. I use a Chinese bamboo steamer that has its own lid. I sit this over a large wok with water in it. The water stays just below the steamer. You could also use a very large pan with a lid or a deep frying pan with a lid. Just set a trivet in the bottom of it and pour in just enough water so it stays below the top of the trivet.

Bring the water for steaming to a rolling boil. Have extra boiling water ready in case you need to replenish it.

In a small pan combine the 2 fl oz/ ¼ cup/ 50 ml of vegetable oil with 2 fl oz/ ¼ cup/ 50 ml of water and bring to a boil. Take it off the flame. Immediately stir in the bicarbonate of soda (baking soda), and pour this mixture into the batter. Stir to mix. Divide the batter into 2 equal portions and pour 1 portion into a cake tin. Set the baking tin in your steamer. Cover and steam for about 20 minutes or until a toothpick inserted in the middle comes out clean. Turn off the flame. Carefully, remove the cake tin from the steamer using two sets of tongs or oven mittens. Let the *dhokla* cool for 10–15 minutes. (Meanwhile, start steaming the second portion.) Now cut it into 1-in/ 2.5-cm cubes and remove from the cake tin.

When both batches of *dhoklas* have been cooked and cut, heat the 3 tbs/ 45 ml of oil in a large frying pan over a medium flame. When very hot, put in the whole black mustard seeds and the sesame seeds. When the seeds start to pop, put in the whole red chillies. Stir them around once or twice and then spoon out the oil and spices over the *dhokla* squares as evenly as you can. Cover with plastic film so the *dhoklas* do not dry out. Garnish with fresh coriander and coconut just before you eat. Serve warm or at room temperature.

4 tbs/ 60 ml chopped fresh green coriander (Chinese parsley)

2–3 tbs/ 30–45 ml grated fresh coconut (p. 145), optional

RICES AND BREADS

Saday Chaval

PLAIN RICE

METHOD

Put the rice in a bowl and wash in several changes of water. Drain. Leave to soak in 2 pints/ 5 cups/ 1.15 litres of water for 30 minutes. Drain thoroughly.

Put the drained rice and 1 pint/ 2 ⅔ cups/ 600 ml of water in a heavy pan and bring to a boil. Cover with a very tight-fitting lid, turn heat to very, very low and cook for 25 minutes. Take the rice pan off the flame and let it rest, still covered and undisturbed, for another 10 minutes.

SERVES 6

Basmati or any long-grain rice measured to the 15 fl oz/ 2 cup/ 450 ml level in a glass measuring jug

Tomato Palak Bhat

RICE WITH TOMATOES AND SPINACH

SERVES 6
———

Basmati or any long-grain rice, measured to the ¾ pint/ 2 cup 450 ml/ mark in a glass measuring jug
———
1 x 10-oz/ 275-g packet of frozen leaf spinach
———
9 oz/ 250 g, 2 small tomatoes
———
3 tbs/ 45 ml vegetable oil
———
2 ½ oz/ 65 g, 1 small onion peeled, cut in half and then cut crosswise into very thin slices
———
¼ tsp ground turmeric
———
1 tsp/ 5 ml roasted, ground coriander and cumin seed mixture (p. 148)
———
1 tsp/ 5 ml salt
———

H ere is one of those wonderful rice dishes that I can eat all by itself, accompanied, at times, by just plain yoghurt and a pickle. You will find that a thin crust might form at the bottom of your pan after you finish cooking. Do not throw it away. It tastes quite wonderful and should be eaten!

Frozen spinach leaves work very well here. Use fresh spinach if you prefer. This particular recipe comes from the Bene Israel community – a Jewish group that settled in Maharashtra centuries ago.

METHOD

Wash the rice in several changes of water and drain. Add enough water to cover by 1 in/ 2.5 cm. Set aside for 30 minutes.

Cook the spinach according to package directions in just 4 fl oz/ ½ cup/ 125 ml of water. It should be tender and have no liquid left. (Fresh spinach may be cooked the same way.) Chop up the spinach very, very finely. Chop the tomatoes finely.

Heat the oil in a heavy pan over a medium-high flame. When hot, put in the onion. Stir and fry until the onion is nicely browned. Add the rice and turn the heat to medium. Stir and sauté the rice for 2 minutes. Now put in the spinach, tomatoes, turmeric, the roasted coriander and cumin seed mixture and salt. Stir gently to mix and keep stirring for 1 minute. Now add ¾ pint/ 2 cups/ 450 ml of water and bring to a boil. Cover very tightly, turn heat to very low and cook for 25 minutes. Remove cover and stir the rice gently, leaving the crust on the very bottom alone. Cover and cook on a very low heat for another 10 minutes.

Yakhni Pullao

RICE COOKED IN AN AROMATIC BROTH

T his is a simplified version of the more classic meat *pullaos*. It requires a rich stock made either with lamb (bones are good for this) or with chicken or a combination of the two.

You could serve this mild *pullao* with most Indian and Western meals.

METHOD

Wash the rice in several changes of water. Drain and put in a bowl. Add about 2 pints/ 5 cups/ 1.1 litres of water and leave to soak for 30 minutes. Drain the rice and leave in a strainer for 20 minutes.

Meanwhile, put the stock, one whole onion, garlic, ginger, peppercorns, cardamom pods, cumin seeds, coriander seeds, fennel seeds, cinnamon and bay leaves into a pan and bring to a simmer. Cover, lower the heat and simmer for 30 minutes. Strain, squeezing out as much liquid as possible. You should end up with 1 pint/ 2½ cups/ 600 ml of liquid. If you have more just boil it down to get the exact amount.

Cut the other onion in half lengthwise and then cut crosswise into fine half rings. Heat the oil in a heavy-based pan over a medium flame. When hot, put in the sliced onion. Stir and fry until the onions brown nicely. Add the rice and the salt. Stir and sauté the rice gently without breaking any grains for 2–3 minutes. Turn the heat down if the rice begins to catch. Now add the flavoured stock and bring to a boil. Cover tightly (use a sheet of foil between the pan and the lid, if necessary), turn the heat to very low and cook for 25 minutes.

SERVES 6

Basmati or any other long-grain rice, measuring to the 15 fl oz/ 2 cup/ 425 ml level in a glass measuring jug

1½ pints/ 4 cups/ 900 ml lamb or chicken stock or a combination of the two

2 medium-sized onions, peeled

2 cloves garlic, peeled

1-in/ 2.5-cm cube fresh ginger, peeled

1 tsp/ 5 ml whole black peppercorns

8 whole cardamom pods

1 tsp/ 5 ml whole cumin seeds

2 tsp/ 10 ml whole coriander seeds

1 tsp/ 5 ml whole fennel seeds

1-in/ 2.5-cm cinnamon stick

2 bay leaves

1 tsp/ 5 ml salt

4 tbs/ 60 ml vegetable oil

Bhopali Matar Gajar Pullao

BHOPALI PILAF WITH PEAS AND CARROTS

SERVES 6

Basmati or other long-
grain rice measured to
the 15 fl oz/ 2 cup/
450 ml mark in a glass
measuring jug

1 ½-in/ 4-cm cube of
fresh ginger, peeled and
coarsely chopped

6–8 large cloves garlic,
peeled and coarsely
chopped

3 ½ oz/ 8.5 cm, medium-
sized onion, peeled

4 tbs/ ⅓ cup/ 60 ml
vegetable oil or *ghee*
(see p. 151)

4 whole cloves

1 large, whole black
cardamom pod

1-in/ 2.5-cm cinnamon
stick

2 bay leaves

¼ tsp whole black cumin
seeds

½-in/ 1-cm, small piece
of whole mace

2 ½ oz/ 65 g, 2 small
carrots, peeled and cut
roughly into the same
size as the peas

4 ½ oz/ 1 cup/ 115 g
shelled peas, fresh or
defrosted if frozen

1 tsp/ 5 ml salt

There are many versions of this delicious pilaf in Bhopal. You can, for example, leave out the peas and carrots. If you cannot find black cardamom, substitute 3 green or white pods.

METHOD

Pick over the rice and wash it in several changes of water. Drain. Put the rice in a bowl and cover with 2 pints/ 5 cups/ 1.15 litres of water. Leave to soak for 30 minutes. Drain thoroughly.

Put the ginger, garlic and and 1 tbs/ 15 ml of water into the container of a food processor or blender. Blend until you have a paste.

Cut the onion in half lengthwise, and then cut crosswise into very fine half rings. Heat the oil in a heavy pan over a medium-high flame. When very hot, put in the cloves, black cardamom, cinnamon, bay leaves, black cumin seeds and mace. Stir once and put in the onion slices. Stir and fry until the onion slices turn reddish-brown. Now put in the ginger-garlic paste. Fry for 2 minutes. Put in the carrots and peas. Stir and fry for 1 minute. Now put in the drained rice and the salt. Lower the flame a bit. Stir and fry the rice for 2–3 minutes. Now put in 1 pint/ 2½ cups/ 600 ml of water and bring to a boil. Cover very tightly, turn the heat to very low and cook gently for 25 minutes.

Masuru Anna

YOGHURT RICE

This is always served at room temperature and may, at Western meals, be served as a rice salad and at Indian meals with Chettinad Fried Chicken and Green Beans with Coconut.

METHOD

Pick over the rice and wash it in several changes of water. Drain. Cover it by about 2 in/ 5 cm of water and leave to soak for 20–30 minutes. Drain.

While the rice is soaking, put the yoghurt in a bowl and add the salt. Beat lightly with a fork or whisk until it is smooth and creamy.

Bring 5 pints/ 12 cups/ 3 litres of water to a rolling boil in a big pan. Drop in the rice, stir and allow the water to come to a boil. Boil vigorously for about 12 minutes or until the rice is not only cooked but is slightly soft. Drain and put in a bowl. Add the yoghurt immediately, while the rice is still hot, and mix gently.

Chop the green chilli very, very finely. Cut the ginger into very fine slices. Stack a few of the slices at a time over each other and cut them first into very fine strips and then cut the strips into minute dice.

Heat the oil in a small frying pan or small pan over a medium flame. When hot, put in the mustard seeds. As soon as the mustard seeds begin to pop, put in the *urad dal*. When the *dal* turns red, put in the curry leaves and red chillies. When the red chillies start to darken, lift up the frying pan and pour its contents over the rice. Sprinkle the green chilli, ginger and fresh green coriander (Chinese parsley) over the rice as well and mix. Do not refrigerate. Serve the dish at room temperature.

SERVES 4

6 oz/ 1 cup/ 75 g long-grain rice

8 fl oz/ 1 cup/ 250 ml plain yoghurt

¾ tsp/ 4 ml salt

1–2 fresh, hot green chillies

½-in/ 1-cm cube of fresh ginger, peeled

1 tbs/ 15 ml vegetable oil

½ tsp/ 2.5 ml whole black mustard seeds

⅛ tsp skinned *urad dal* (p. 150)

8–10 fresh or dried curry leaves

2 dried hot red chillies

1 tbs/ 15 ml finely chopped fresh green coriander (Chinese parsley)

Hyderabadi Qabooli

HYDERABADI PILAF OF RICE AND SPLIT PEAS

SERVES 6

2 ½ oz/ ½ cup/ 65 g skinned *chana dal* or yellow split peas (p. 149)

Basmati or any other long-grain rice, measured to the ¾ pint/ 2 cup/ 450 ml mark in a glass measuring jug

½ tsp/ 2.5 ml ground turmeric

4 tbs/ 60 ml vegetable oil

4 ½ oz/ 115 g, 1 large onion, peeled, cut in half lengthwise and then cut crosswise into very fine half rings

2 tsp/ 10 ml finely grated, peeled fresh ginger

1 tsp/ 5 ml finely crushed garlic

5 tbs/ 75 ml plain yoghurt

salt

⅛–¼ tsp red chilli powder (cayenne pepper)

Although a dish of rice and beans, this is a very elegant one – indeed, the first time I had it in Hyderabad, it was at a very lavish and grand banquet.

You could serve it with any meat dish and some nice, simple vegetable, such as Carrots with Dill. Relishes and salads, and yoghurt dishes also, go particularly well with this pilaf.

METHOD

Pick over the *chana dal* and wash it in several changes of water. Leave to soak in enough water to cover it by 3 in/ 7.5 cm for 1½ hours.

Pick over the rice and wash it in several changes of water. Leave to soak in enough water to cover it by 2 in/ 5 cm for 30 minutes. Drain.

Put the *dal* and its soaking liquid into a pan. Add ¼ tsp of the turmeric and bring to a boil. Cover, leaving the lid slightly ajar, turn the heat down and simmer for about 30 minutes or until it is almost tender but the grains are still whole. Drain.

Heat the oil in a non-stick frying pan over a medium-high flame. When hot, put in the onions. Stir and fry them until they are a rich, reddish-brown colour and crisp. Remove with a slotted spoon and spread out on a plate lined with absorbent kitchen paper (paper towels). Put the ginger and garlic into the same oil. Stir and fry until lightly browned. Now put in the remaining ¼ tsp of turmeric and 1 tbs/ 15 ml of the yoghurt. Stir and fry until most of the liquid in the yoghurt evaporates and the remaining particles brown lightly. Add the remaining yoghurt, 1 tbs/ 15 ml at a time, and cook in the same way. Now put in the drained *dal*, ½ tsp/ 2.5 ml salt and the chilli powder (cayenne pepper). Stir to mix. Sauté the *dal* for 1 minute.

Heat the oven to 325°F/ 170°C/ gas mark 3.

Bring 5 pints/ 12 cups/ 3 litres of water to a rolling boil. Add 1 tbs/ 15 ml of salt and stir. Now put in the drained rice and bring to a boil again. Boil vigorously for 5 minutes or until the rice is about three-quarters cooked. It should retain a slim, hard, inner core. Drain the rice and empty half of it into a wide, oven-proof casserole-type pan. Cover the rice with the cooked *dal*. Cover the dal with the remaining rice. Spread the *ghee* and the browned onions over the rice. Sprinkle the lemon juice and milk, fresh coriander (Chinese parsley), mint, green chillies and *garam masala* over the top. Cover tightly, first with foil and then with a lid and place in the oven for 30 minutes.

Stir gently to mix before serving.

2 tbs/ 30 ml *ghee*
(p. 151) or 1 oz/ 25 g/
2 tbs unsalted butter,
cut into small pieces

2 tbs/ 30 ml lemon juice

2 tbs/ 30 ml milk

1 tbs/ 15 ml finely
chopped fresh, green
coriander (Chinese
parsley)

1 tbs/ 15 ml finely
chopped fresh mint

2–4 fresh green chillies,
very finely chopped

½ tsp/ 2.5 ml *garam
masala* (p. 151)

Appams

KERALA HOPPERS – RICE PANCAKES

**MAKES ABOUT 16
APPAMS**

———

1 lb 2 oz/ 3 cups/ 500 g
long-grain rice such as
Carolina (perfumed rice,
such as Basmati is not
suitable)

———

14 fl oz/ 1 ¾ cups/
400 ml unsweetened
coconut milk, fresh or
tinned (p. 146)

———

1 ½ tsp/ 7.5 ml active
dry yeast granules

———

3 tbs/ 45 ml sugar

———

3 medium-sized eggs, at
room temperature

———

½ tsp/ 2.5 ml salt

———

about 4 fl oz/ ½ cup/
125 ml extra warm water
or coconut milk

———

about 6 tbs/ ½ cup/
90 ml vegetable oil

———

I have often said that if a French crêpe were to marry a crumpet or an English muffin, they would probably become the proud parents of *appams*. *Appams* are a special kind of pancake made out of a leavened rice batter. They are thick, soft, white and spongy in the centre and crisp and lace-like along their golden edges.

There is nothing quite as gorgeous as steaming hot *appams* and they remain one of my favourite Indian pancakes. What makes them especially attractive is that they are really very easy to make. If you can make a crêpe, you can make an *appam*. Time *is* required for the soaking of rice and the fermentation of the batter but this is time which the cook can spend twiddling his or her thumbs.

In Kerala, a special two-handled cast-iron wok is used for making *appams*. I do not happen to have such a utensil and I find my well seasoned, large, Chinese wok perfectly adequate. If you do not have a wok, use a crêpe pan. You will not get the traditional *appam* form but you will still end up with a good pancake. Also, I find that my electric blender makes a better batter than my food processor. The recipe here is not the traditional one requiring the hand-pounding of two different types of rice, toddy for fermentation and cooked rice paste for added texture. This is a much simplified recipe worked out by a Keralite in a Washington DC kitchen. The results, you will find, are superb.

There are many ways to eat an *appam:* smear it when hot with butter and jam or honey and eat for breakfast or dessert; put fine ground sugar and thick coconut milk on it and eat it with a meal or as a snack or as a dessert; use it as a bread and eat it with Chicken Stew or Green Chilli Chicken. The *appam* seems designed to absorb juices whether they be buttery and sweet or hot and savoury. The batter for *appam* is most amenable. It lends itself to busy schedules with the utmost flexibility. Once you have made the batter you may refrigerate it overnight and use it the next morning. You can also, wonder of wonders, freeze it. Just allow it to thaw completely and come to room temperature before you start cooking.

METHOD

Put the rice in a bowl and wash it in several changes of water. Drain. Add enough water to the rice to cover it by 1 ½ in/ 4 cm and leave to soak for at least 8 hours or overnight.

Drain the rice and put it in a blender. Add the 14 fl oz/ 1 ¾ cups/ 400 ml of coconut milk and blend until you have a fine paste. There will be very fine granules in the paste but that is as it should be. Empty the paste out into a bowl.

Put the yeast and 1 tbs/ 15 ml of the sugar into a cup. Add the 4 tbs/ 60 ml of warm water and mix. (The water should be about 100°-115°F/ 38°-46°C). Set aside for about 10 minutes for the fermenting action to start. Add the yeast mixture to the batter in the bowl and mix it in. Cover the bowl with a plate and leave it in a warm place for 6 hours.

Beat the eggs lightly. Add the salt and the remaining sugar. Mix. Add this mixture to the batter. Stir. Add about 4 fl oz/ 125 ml/ ½ cup of warm water or coconut milk to the batter to produce a consistency perhaps just a little bit thicker than a crêpe batter.

Get everything ready for making the *appams:* set up your wok and keep its cover handy; you will need a pastry brush or a wad of cloth; put the oil in a small bowl; keep near you the bowl of batter, a measure or ladle that will hold a tiny bit less than 3 fl oz/ ⅓ cup/ 85 ml, and a spatula that works well in the wok; you will also need a deep dish to hold the *appams* as they get made and some foil to wrap them in if you are not eating them immediately.

Put on a low flame under the wok and let it heat a bit. Dip the pastry brush or the cloth wad in the bowl of oil and brush a 7-in/ 18-cm circumference with it in the centre of the wok. Stir the batter gently. Ladle just a little less than 3 fl oz/ ⅓ cup/ 85 ml of batter into the centre of the wok. Quickly pick up the wok by its two handles (if it has only one handle, wear an oven glove (mitten) and put your second hand where the second handle might have been). Tilt the wok around, just as you would for crêpes, so the batter covers about a 6 in/ 15 cm diameter. Cover and cook for about 3 ½ minutes on a low heat. The bottom and edges of the *appam* should barely turn golden and the centre should be pale and spongy. Eat immediately, if possible. Otherwise put the *appam* in a deep dish, cover and make the rest of the *appams*.

Leftover *appams* may be wrapped tightly in foil and refrigerated. Heat foil packet in a moderately hot oven 400°F/ 200°C/ gas mark 6 for about 10 minutes.

Roti

FLAT WHOLEWHEAT BREAD

METHOD

Put the flour in a bowl. Slowly add enough water so that you will be able to gather the flour together and make a soft dough. You will need about 6½ fl oz/ a good ¾ cup/ 190 ml of water. Knead the dough for 7–8 minutes or until it is smooth. Make a ball and put it inside a bowl. Cover the bowl with a damp cloth and set it aside for 30 minutes.

If the dough looks very runny, flour your hands and knead for another few minutes. Form 12 equal balls, dust each one with a little flour, and cover.

Set a *tava*, cast-iron griddle or cast-iron frying pan to heat over a medium-low flame. Allow at least 5 minutes for that. Keep some extra flour for dusting near you. Remove a ball of dough and flatten it between the palms of your hands. Dust it on both sides with flour. Roll it out, as thinly and evenly as you can, aiming for a 5 ½-in/ 13.5-cm circle. When the griddle is hot, slap the *roti* on to its heated surface. Cook for about 1 minute or until soft bubbles begin to form. Turn the *roti* over. (Most Indians use their hands to do this.) Cook for ½ minute on the second side. If you have a gas cooker, light a second burner on a medium flame and put the *roti* directly on it. Using tongs with rounded ends, rotate the *roti* so that all areas are exposed to the shooting flames. Take 5 seconds to do this. Turn the *roti* over and repeat for about 3 seconds. The *roti* should puff up. Put the *roti* on a plate and cover with a clean tea towel (dish towel). Make all *rotis* this way. If you have an electric stove, place the griddle and *roti* under a grill (broiler) for a few seconds, until the *roti* puffs up. Serve hot.

MAKES 12 ROTIS

8 oz/ 2 cups/ 225 g *chapati* flour (p. 144) or 4 oz/ 1 cup/ 100 g sieved wholewheat flour mixed with 4 oz/ 1 cup/ 100 g plain white flour

additional flour for dusting

Paratha

FLAKY PAN BREAD

MAKES 8 PARATHAS

½ lb/ 1¾ cups/ 250 g
plain white or
unbleached white flour

½ lb/ 1¾ cups/ 250 g
wheatmeal or
wholewheat flour, sifted

1 tsp/ 5 ml salt

extra flour, wheatmeal
or white, for dusting

about 8 fl oz/ 1 cup/
250 ml ghee (p. 151) or
melted butter

One of the best unleavened breads of India, these Hyderabadi *parathas* should be cooked on an Indian *tava*, a slightly concave cast-iron plate, or else in a cast-iron frying pan. They can be served with kebabs, with Hyderabadi or North Indian sauced meats and all the *bhaji*-type vegetable dishes such as Cauliflower with dried Chillies and Mustard Seeds, Spicy Potatoes, Stir-fried Aubergine (Eggplant) and Stuffed Okra.

If you have access to *chapati* flour (p. 144), available at Indian grocers, you may use 1 lb/ 450 g of it instead of the two suggested flours.

METHOD

Put the two types of flour and salt into a bowl. Slowly add about ½ pint/ 1¼ cups/ 300 ml of water to get as soft a dough as possible. Knead the dough for 10 minutes. Cover and set aside for 4 hours.

Knead the dough again, using extra flour if it is sticky. Divide the dough into 8 balls. Set 7 aside and work on the eighth.

Set a *tava* or cast-iron frying pan to heat over a lowish flame.

Dust your work surface with flour. Put 1 ball of dough on it and flatten it into a patty. Roll it out until it is about 7 in/ 18 cm in diameter. Smear the surface of the *paratha* with about ½ tsp/ 2.5 ml of *ghee*. Now lightly dust a little flour over the *ghee*. Starting from the edge farthest away from you, begin rolling the *paratha* tightly towards you. You will now have a long 'snake'. Coil the 'snake' around itself tightly, spiralling upwards. Push down the spiral to form a patty. Dust the patty lightly with flour and roll it out into a round that is about ⅛ in/ 0.25 cm thick and roughly 7 ½ in/ 20.5 cm in diameter.

When the *tava* is well heated, slap the *paratha* onto it. Let it just sit for 30 seconds or so. Now lift it up slightly and dribble about 1 tsp/ 5 ml of *ghee* under it. Make a wad out of some absorbent kitchen paper (paper towel) and press down on the *paratha*, turning it slightly each time you do this. Cook the *paratha* this way for 2–3 minutes or until the bottom has reddish-brown patches. Dribble 1 tsp/ 5 ml of *ghee* on top of the *paratha* and turn it over. Press again with the wad of absorbent kitchen paper (kitchen towel), turning the *paratha* a bit each time you do so. Cook the second side for about 3 minutes or until it too has reddish-brown patches. When the *paratha* is done, wrap it quickly in aluminium foil. Make all *parathas* this way.

Note: the *parathas* may be stacked together wrapped in aluminium foil. This entire wrapped packet can then be heated in the oven set at 350°F/ 180°C/ gas mark 4 for 10–15 minutes, just before you eat.

Shirmal

FLAKY OVEN BREAD

**MAKES 8 BREADS AND
SERVES 8**

1 lb/ 3 ¾ cup/ 450 g
plain white flour

1 tsp/ 5 ml salt

2 tsp/ 10 ml sugar

3 ½ oz/ 90 g/
7 tbs *ghee* (p. 151) or
clarified butter

½ pint/ 1 ¼ cup/ 300 ml
milk

flour, for dusting

an extra ¼ pint/ ⅔ cup/
150 ml milk with a few
strands of saffron
soaked in it for 1–2
hours

8 tsp/ 40 ml extra *ghee*
or clarified butter

Versions of this unleavened bread are made throughout Muslim India. In the bazaars of Lucknow, the bread bakes in a *tandoor*-like oven, stuck to its very hot, cast-iron walls. When it is done, it is sprinkled lightly with saffron milk to keep it moist. These days, with saffron being so expensive, food colouring is used and the *shirmals* wind up looking the same colour as *tandoori* chicken – an unnatural orange-red! I think it is best to use very little saffron – or none at all, rather than food colouring. You could smear some melted *ghee* on the *shirmals* instead of sprinkling them with saffron water, if you prefer, or you could do both, as I have done. *Shirmals* may be served with most Indian meals and go particularly well with lamb dishes, as well as vegetables, *dals* and relishes. I have even been known to eat left-over *shirmals* for breakfast with cheese or with butter and jam!

METHOD

Put the flour, salt and sugar into a large bowl. Add the *ghee* and rub it into the flour with your fingers. Now begin to add the milk slowly. Try to form a ball. Keep adding the milk until you can form a ball. Start kneading, adding a little more milk as you do so. Keep kneading as you incorporate all the milk (*not* the saffron milk). Knead until the dough is soft and very smooth. Put the dough in a clean bowl. Cover and set aside for 2 hours. Knead again and set aside for another hour.

Heat the oven to 500°F/ 240°C/ gas mark 9 and put a large, cast-iron frying pan on a shelf set

in the middle of the oven to heat as well. Heat
your grill (broiler) also.

Knead the dough again and divide into 8 equal
balls. Flatten the balls into smooth patties and
set aside. Keep seven covered as you work on the
eighth.

Dust your work surface with a little flour and
put the patty on it. Dust its top with flour. Now roll
it out until it is about 6-in/ 15-cm in diameter and
about ¼-in/ 0.5-cm thick. Prick the *shirmal* all
over with a fork or with the tip of a knife.

Lift the *shirmal* carefully onto the spread palm
of your hand. Open the oven and slap the bread
into the heated frying pan. Bake for about 2 minutes. Now dip the tips of your fingers in the saffron
milk, open the oven door, and sprinkle just what
clings to your fingertips on to the *shirmal*. Do this
by flicking your fingers. Do this one more time and
close the oven door. Cook the *shirmal* for a total of
about 5 minutes. It should develop a few brown
spots on top and brown a bit underneath. Take it
out and put it under your grill (broiler) for about
10 seconds.

Now flick a few more drops of saffron milk on
it and, if you like, smear about ½ tsp/ 2.5 ml of *ghee*
over it. Wrap immediately in aluminium foil or in
a very lightly dampened tea towel (dish towel).
Make all the *shirmals* this way.

Papar or Papadum

DAL WAFERS

C alled *papadum* in South India and *papar* in the
North, these thin wafers are generally made
out of split peas, such as *urad dal* or split mung
beans, *moong dal*, though they could also be made
out of potatoes or sago. They are served at nearly all vegetarian meals in India. Bengalis eat them
towards the end of a meal with chutney; South-
erners are known to crush them and eat them with
rice, yoghurt and pickles while North Indians
often serve them as appetizers with drinks. *Papadums* are bought partially prepared. All you have to
do is cook them. There are two basic methods to
choose from: frying or roasting. The traditional
method is to deep fry them. This allows the *papadums* to expand to their fullest and turn very light
and airy. This method does however, leave those
who are nibbling the wafers with slightly greasy fingers. The second method is to roast the *papadums*
directly over or under a flame. This way you end
up with clean fingers and the *papadums* are less
calorific. But the *papadums* do not expand as much
and remain denser than the fried ones.

Papadums may be bought plain, dotted with
black pepper, dotted with red pepper or flavoured
with garlic.

You may serve *papadums* with drinks or with
any Indian meal.

Frying method

4 papadums

vegetable oil for deep
frying

METHOD

Break each *papadum* into 2 pieces.

Pour enough oil into a wok or frying pan to
come to a depth of ¾ in/ 2 cm. Set the oil to heat
over a medium flame. When hot, drop in a *papad-*

um half. Within seconds it will sizzle and expand. Remove the *papadum* with a slotted spoon and drain on absorbent kitchen paper (paper towels). Cook all the *papadums* this way.

Papadums should retain their yellowish colour and not brown. They should also cook very fast. Adjust your heat if necessary.

METHOD

Preheat your grill (broiler).

Put 1 *papadum* on a rack and place it about 3 in/7.5 cm away from the source of heat. Watch it carefully. It will expand in seconds. It will also pale and develop a few bubbles. Turn it over and expose the second side to the flame for a few seconds. Watch it all the time and do not let it brown or burn. Remove from the grill (broiler) when done. Make all the *papadums* this way. (When making *papadums* under a grill (broiler) it is not always necessary to turn them over. You will just have to use your own judgment here.)

If you happen to have a toasted sandwich maker (electric toaster oven) you may make your *papadums* in that. Just as you would under a grill (broiler). That is what, in fact, I do in my own house.

Roasting method
—

4 papadums
—

Poori

DEEP-FRIED PUFFY BREAD

🐘

**MAKES 12 POORIS AND
SERVES 4**

4 oz/ 1 cup/ 100 g
sieved, wheatmeal
(wholewheat) flour

4 oz/ 1 cup/ 100 g plain
flour (unbleached all-
purpose flour)

½ tsp/ 2.5 ml salt

2 tbs/ 30 ml vegetable
oil, plus more for deep
frying

3 ½ fl oz/ ½ cup/ 120 ml
water or milk

These deep-fried breads puff up in hot oil like
balloons. They are crispy-soft and may be
eaten with almost all Indian meats, vegetables
and split peas.

It is most economical – and safe – to make
pooris in a wok or an Indian *karhai*. You may use
8 oz/ 2 cups/ 225 g *chapati* flour to make the *pooris*.
If you cannot find it, use the combination suggested here.

METHOD

Put the two flours and salt in a bowl. Dribble the
2 tbs/ 30 ml of oil over the top. Rub the oil in with
your fingers so the mixture resembles coarse breadcrumbs. Slowly add the water to form a stiff ball
of dough. Empty the ball on to a clean work surface. Knead it for 10–12 minutes or until it is
smooth. Form a ball. Rub about ¼ tsp of oil on the
ball and slip it into a plastic bag. Set it aside for 30
minutes.

Knead the dough again, and divide it into 12
equal balls. Keep 11 of them covered while you
work with the twelfth. Flatten this ball and roll it
out into a 5–5 ½-in/ 12.5–13.5-cm circle. If you have
the space, roll out all the *pooris* and keep them in
a single layer, covered with cling film (plastic
wrap).

Over a medium flame, set about 1 in/ 2.5 cm of
oil to heat in a wok, *karhai* or small, deep frying
pan. Let it get very, very hot. Meanwhile, line a
platter with absorbent kitchen paper (paper towel).
Lift up one *poori* and lay it carefully over the surface of the hot oil. It might sink to the bottom but

it should rise in seconds and begin to sizzle. Using the back of a slotted spoon, push the *poori* gently into the oil with tiny, swift strokes. Within seconds, the *poori* will puff up. Turn it over and cook the second side for about 10 seconds. Remove it with a slotted spoon and put it on the platter. Make all the *pooris* this way. The first layer on the platter may be covered with a layer of absorbent kitchen paper (paper towel). More *pooris* can then be spread over the top. Serve the *pooris* hot.

CHUTNEYS, RELISHES, SALADS AND DRINKS

Lassi

A YOGHURT DRINK

O ne of the few drinks, other than water, that is drunk with meals in India. Lassi is very popular at breakfast, lunch and as a snack. It can be sweet or salty. If you wish to make sweet lassi, do not put in the salt or cumin. Instead, put in as much sugar as you like.

METHOD

Combine all the ingredients in the container of an electric blender and blend for 3 seconds. If you do not have a blender, put the yoghurt in a bowl. Beat with a fork or whisk until smooth and creamy. Slowly add the water, beating as you do so. Add all the other ingredients and mix.

SERVES 2

4 fl oz/ ½ cup/ 125 ml plain yoghurt

½ pint/ 1 ¼ cup/ 300 ml ice-cold water

½ tsp/ 2.5 ml ground roasted cumin seeds

¼ tsp salt

¼ tsp finely crumbled, dried mint, optional

Dahi Ki Chutney

YOGHURT CHUTNEY

SERVES 6

¾ pint/ 2 cups/ 450 ml
plain yoghurt

¾ tsp/ 4 ml salt

---

freshly ground black
pepper

---

3 tbs/ 45 ml very finely
chopped onions

---

1 tsp/ 5 ml very finely
grated, peeled fresh
ginger

---

1 tsp/ 5 ml very finely
crushed garlic

---

2 tbs/ 30 ml very finely
chopped fresh mint
leaves

---

2 tbs/ 30 ml very finely
chopped fresh green
coriander (Chinese
parsley)

---

pinch red chilli powder
(cayenne pepper)

H ere is a simple yoghurt relish that seems to appear at all meals in Hyderabad.

METHOD

Put the yoghurt in a bowl. Beat lightly with a fork or a whisk until smooth and creamy. Add all the other ingredients except the red chilli powder and mix well. Sprinkle the chilli powder over the top as a garnish.

Cheera Pachadi
SPINACH AND YOGHURT

T he *pachadis* of Kerala may be made with all manner of vegetables and fruit, including okra, pumpkin, semi-ripe pineapples and green mangoes. They add sparkle and zest to meals, serving as a cross between a relish and a vegetable dish.

Pachadis go well with most Indian meals, and especially well with rice.

METHOD

Heat the oil in a wok or a medium-sized frying pan over a medium flame. When hot, put in the cumin seeds and *urad dal*. As soon as the *dal* turns reddish, put in the curry leaves and red chilli. When the red chilli darkens (this just takes a second), put in the shallots and green chillies. Stir and sauté until the shallots turn golden. Add the coconut and stir once. Now put in the spinach and salt. Turn the heat down a bit. Stir and sauté the spinach until it is tender, adding a little more water if you think there is any danger of the spinach browning.

Put the yoghurt in a bowl. Beat lightly with a fork or a whisk until it is smooth and creamy. Add the contents of the wok or frying pan. Mix well and serve at room temperature or cold.

SERVES 6

5 tbs/ 75 ml vegetable oil

1 tsp/ 5 ml whole cumin seeds

1 tsp/ 5 ml skinned *urad dal* (p. 150)

8–10 fresh or dried curry leaves

1 whole, hot, dried red chilli, broken into 2–3 pieces

4 tbs/ ⅓ cup/ 60 ml peeled and finely sliced shallots

2–3 fresh, hot green chillies, sliced into very fine rounds

1 oz/ ⅓ cup/ 25 g grated fresh coconut (p. 145)

5 oz/ 2 well packed cups/ 150 g spinach leaves, finely sliced

about ½ tsp/ 2.5 ml salt

¾ pint/ 2 cups/ 450 ml plain yoghurt

Vendakay Pachadi
OKRA WITH YOGHURT

SERVES 4–6

1 tsp/ 5 ml whole, black
mustard seeds

9 oz/ 250 g fresh okra

6 tbs/ ½ cup/ 90 ml
vegetable oil

¾ pint/ 2 cups/ 450 ml
plain yoghurt

½ tsp/ 2.5 ml peeled
and finely grated fresh
ginger

½ tsp/ 2.5 ml salt

1 hot, fresh green chilli,
finely chopped

pinch of ground
asafetida (optional)

¼ tsp whole black
mustard seeds

10 fresh or dried curry
leaves

1 dried, hot red chilli,
broken into 2 pieces

T his *pachadi*, similar to the spinach one on the previous page, is made with fried okra. I am including it only because I find it utterly delicious and simple to make. You could also make it with pumpkin, as my hostess did. Just boil cubes of pumpkin in a little water flavoured with turmeric and red chilli powder (cayenne pepper). Boil until the water gets absorbed. Then put the pumpkin pieces into seasoned yoghurt as you would the okra.

METHOD

Put the 1 tsp/ 5 ml of black mustard seeds into the container of an electric coffee grinder or a spice grinder. Grind as fine as possible. Leave in the grinder.

Rinse the okra quickly and pat it dry. Cut off the tip and the top crowns of the okra pods and then cut them crosswise, into ¼-in/ 0.5-cm, thick rounds.

Heat the oil in a wok or frying pan over a medium flame. When hot, put in the okra. Stir and fry until the okra turns reddish brown in parts and is cooked through. Remove the okra with a slotted spoon and put in a plate lined with absorbent kitchen paper (paper towels). Strain off the oil in the pan and save it.

Put the yoghurt in a bowl. Beat it lightly with a fork or a whisk until it is smooth and creamy. Add the ground mustard seeds to the yoghurt as well as the ginger, salt, sugar and green chilli. Mix. Put the okra into the yoghurt and stir it in.

In a small frying pan, heat 2 tbs/ 30 ml of the oil that the okra was fried in over a medium flame.

When hot, put in first the asafetida, then a second later, the whole mustard seeds. As soon as the mustard seeds begin to pop, put in the curry leaves and the red chilli. When the chilli darkens, pour the contents of the frying pan, oil and spices, into the yoghurt. Mix.

Serve at room temperature. You may also let the *pachadi* sit, covered and unrefrigerated, for a day and serve it the following day.

Note: the pieces of red chilli should only be eaten by those who know what they are doing!

Koshimbir I

CUCUMBERS WITH FRESH COCONUT

SERVES 4

SERVES 4
___

2 oz/ 50 g, 4 tbs
roasted, shelled peanuts
___

10 oz/ 1 ½ cups/ 275 g,
2 small or 1 large
chopped cucumber
___

·2 tbs/ 30 ml grated fresh
coconut (p. 145)
___

2 small green chillies,
very finely chopped
___

2 tbs/ 30 ml lemon juice
___

½ tsp/ 2.5 ml sugar
___

½ tsp/ 2.5 ml salt
___

1 tbs/ 15 ml vegetable oil
___

⅛ tsp ground asafetida
___

¼ tsp whole black
mustard seeds
___

⅛ tsp red chilli powder
(cayenne pepper)

K oshimbirs are simple everyday relishes from Maharashtra that are served with most meals. There are many variations. Since I like them all, I have chosen two to put in this book. This relish calls for roasted peanuts. You may use any that you find. Even fried peanuts will do. If they happen to be salted, taste the *koshimbir* just before you add the salt, then put in however much you need.

METHOD

Put the peanuts in a mortar and crush them lightly. You can, if you prefer, chop them coarsely with a knife.

Peel the cucumbers and cut them into ¼-in/ 0.5-cm dice.

In a bowl, combine the peanuts, cucumber, coconut, green chillies, lemon juice, sugar and salt. Mix.

Heat the oil in a small frying pan over a medium flame. When hot, put in first the asafetida, then, a second later, the mustard seeds. As soon as the mustard seeds begin to pop, put in the red chilli powder (cayenne pepper). Lift up the frying pan and tilt it around to stir the spices. Now pour the contents of the pan over the relish. Stir to mix. Serve at room temperature.

Koshimbir II

TOMATO AND ONION WITH YOGHURT

SERVES 4

T his relish, like the last, may be served with most Indian meals.

METHOD

Put the tomato, onion, yoghurt and salt into a bowl and mix.

Heat the oil in a small frying pan over a medium flame. When hot, put in first the asafetida, then, a second later, the mustard seeds. As soon as the mustard seeds begin to pop, put in the red chilli powder (cayenne pepper). Lift up the frying pan, tilting it around gently once to stir its contents and then pour the contents over relish. Stir to mix. Serve at room temperature.

4 oz/ 100 g, 1 medium-sized tomato, cut into ¼-in/ 0.5-cm dice

2 oz/ 50 g, 1 small onion, chopped fine

2 tbs/ 30 ml yoghurt

¼ tsp salt

2 tsp/ 10 ml vegetable oil

pinch ground asafetida (optional)

¼ tsp whole black mustard seeds

⅛ tsp red chilli powder (cayenne pepper)

Sev Ka Raita

YOGHURT WITH APPLE

SERVES 4

½ pint/ ¼ cups/ 300 ml
plain yoghurt

½ tsp/ 2.5 ml roasted
and ground cumin seeds
(p. 148)

⅛ tsp red chilli powder
(cayenne pepper)

¼ tsp finely grated,
peeled fresh ginger

⅓–½ tsp/ 1–2.5 ml salt

about half a big, hard,
somewhat tart apple,
such as a Granny Smith

If you are looking for a cooling relish to serve with spicy Indian dishes, this is it. In the vegetarian households that traditionally serve it, it has a double function – it acts as a refresher and a digestive, both at the same time.

The yoghurt may be mixed with its seasonings well in advance, but the apple should be grated into it just before serving.

METHOD

Put the yoghurt in a bowl. Beat lightly with a fork or a whisk until smooth and creamy. Add the cumin, red chilli powder (cayenne pepper), ginger and salt. Mix. Cover and refrigerate.

Just before serving, peel the apple and core it. Grate it very coarsely, using the largest holes in the grater and mix in with the yoghurt.

Laccha

TOMATO, ONION AND CUCUMBER RELISH

his is a very simple, everyday relish – you could almost call it a salad – that is served with most meals in Delhi.

METHOD

Peel the onion and cut it into paper-thin rounds. Soak in a bowl of icy water for 30 minutes. Drain and pat dry. Separate the rounds into rings.

In a serving plate, arrange the tomato slices in a single or slightly overlapping layer. Arrange the cucumber slices similarly on top of the tomatoes. Scatter the onion rings over the cucumbers. Sprinkle the lemon juice, salt, chilli powder (cayenne pepper), black pepper and cumin over everything. Toss just the onion rings, leaving the bottom layers undisturbed.

SERVES 6

3 oz/ 75 g, 1 medium-sized onion

4 oz/ 100 g, 1 medium-sized tomato, cut into thinnish slices

10 oz/ 275 g, 2 medium-sized cucumbers, peeled and cut into thin slices

2 tbs/ 30 ml lemon juice

½–¾ tsp/ 2.5–4 ml salt

¼–½ tsp red chilli powder (cayenne pepper)

freshly ground black pepper

½ tsp/ 2.5 ml ground roasted cumin seeds (p. 148)

Timator Chutney

TOMATO CHUTNEY

SERVES 6

1-in/ 2.5-cm cube of
ginger, peeled
---

2 tbs/ 30 ml vegetable
oil

½ tsp/ 2.5 ml
panchphoran (p. 154)
---

2 whole, hot, dried red
chillies
---

6 good-sized cloves of
garlic, mashed to a pulp
---

1 lb/ 450 g tomatoes,
chopped
---

1 tsp/ 5 ml salt
---

2 ½ oz/ ½ cup/ 72 g
sugar

4–5 dried apricots, cut
into ½-in/ 1-cm cubes
---

2 whole, fresh hot green
chillies

In Bengal, sweet or sweet and sour chutneys are served after all the main courses and just before dessert as palate cleansers. They are generally accompanied by crisp *papadums*. You may, of course, serve the chutney with almost any Indian meal.

Here is a very easily made, and delicious, chutney whose flavour takes me back to Calcutta's dining rooms in one swift leap. In Bengal, small cubes of dried mango are added towards the end of the cooking period. These are hard to find in the West. I find that dried apricots make a perfectly good substitute.

METHOD

Cut the ginger, crosswise, into very fine slices. Stacking several slices together at a time, cut them into very fine slivers.

Heat the oil in a heavy-based pan over a medium flame. When hot, put in the *panchphoran*. Let the spices sizzle and pop for a few seconds. Now put in the red chillies. Stir once and put in the ginger and garlic. Stir for about 5 seconds. Now put in the tomatoes, salt and sugar. Simmer on a medium to medium-low flame or until the chutney begins to thicken. This may take about 15–20 minutes. Now add the apricot cubes and the green chillies. Simmer and cook on a lowish heat for another 10–15 minutes or until the chutney is thick and has a glazed look. Serve at room temperature.

Note: the chillies should only be eaten by those who know what they are doing.

Kosambri

CUCUMBER SALAD WITH MOONG DAL

T his Mysore-style salad is crisp and refreshing. Nothing is cooked, not even the *dal*. You may serve it with any Indian meal.

METHOD

Pick over the dal and wash it in several changes of water. Leave to soak for 5–8 hours. Drain.

Peel the cucumber and cut it into ¼-in/ 0.5-cm thick slices.

Put the *moong dal*, cucumber, coconut, fresh coriander (Chinese parsley), lemon juice and salt in a bowl. Mix.

Heat the oil in a small frying pan over a medium flame. When hot, put in the mustard seeds. As soon as the mustard seeds begin to pop (this takes just a few seconds), put in the *urad dal*. When the *dal* turns red, put in the red chilli and curry leaves. As soon as the red chilli starts to darken, pour the contents of the frying pan, oil and spices, into a bowl with the salad. Stir to mix and serve at room temperature.

SERVES 4

1 ½ oz/ ¼ cup/ 40 g skinned *moong dal* (p. 149)

7 oz/ 200 g, 2 small or 1 large cucumber

2 tbs/ 30 ml finely grated fresh coconut (p. 145)

2 tbs/ 30 ml chopped fresh green coriander (Chinese parsley)

1 tbs + 1 tsp/ 20 ml lemon juice

½ tsp/ 2.5 ml salt

2 tsp/ 10 ml vegetable oil

¼ tsp whole black mustard seeds

¼ tsp skinned *urad dal*, picked over (p. 150)

1 whole, dried hot red chilli, broken into 2 pieces

5–6 fresh or dried curry leaves (p. 149)

Mangay Pajji

MANGO SALAD

SERVES 4–6

about 1 lb/ 450 g,
1 large ripe mango or
two smaller ones

1 tsp/ 5 ml whole black
mustard seeds

8 fl oz/ 1 cup/ 250 ml
plain yoghurt

1 fresh hot green chilli,
very finely chopped or
⅛ – ¼ tsp red chilli
powder (cayenne
pepper)

1 tbs/ 15 ml finely grated
fresh coconut (p. 145)
(optional)

1 tsp/ 5 ml sugar

¼ tsp salt

2 tsp/ 10 ml vegetable
oil

1 whole dried hot red
chilli

1 small shallot, peeled
and thinly sliced

This particular recipe comes from a Coorgi family. The salad is sweet and sour and can act as a delicious cooler at all Indian meals.

METHOD

Peel the mango. Cut the flesh into ½-in/ 1-cm cubes.

Put ¾ tsp/ 4 ml of the mustard seeds into the container of a clean coffee grinder or other spice grinder. Grind.

Put the yoghurt in a bowl. Beat lightly with a fork or whisk until smooth and creamy. Add the ground mustard seeds, the green chilli, coconut (if using it), sugar and salt. Add the mango and stir it in.

Heat the oil in a small frying pan over a medium flame. When hot, put in the remaining ¼ tsp of mustard seeds. As soon as the mustard seeds begin to pop (this just takes a few seconds), put in the red chilli. When it starts to darken, put in the shallot. Stir and fry the shallot until it gets slightly brown. Now empty the contents of the frying pan into the bowl with the mango. Stir to mix and serve at room temperature or cold.

SOME BASICS OF INDIAN COOKING

Dried powder and slices made from sour unripe mangoes. My recipes call for only ground (ie, powdered) *amchoor*. Amchoor gives foods a slightly sweet sourness. If unavailable, lemon juice may be substituted.

AMCHOOR

A somewhat smelly brown resin used mainly for its digestive properties and its truffle-like flavour. It is available both in lump form and as a grainy powder. The lump is supposed to be purer. Break off a small chip with a hammer and crush it between two sheets of paper to make your own powder, if you wish.

ASAFETIDA (HEENG)

A fine aromatic, long grain rice grown in the foothills of the Himalaya mountains. If unavailable, any fine long grain rice may be substituted. Basmati rice should be carefully picked over and washed in several changes of water before being cooked.

BASMATI RICE

See *Garam Masala*.

BENGALI GARAM MASALA

An aromatic spice, generally sold in its pod. The green-coloured pods are more aromatic than the plumper, bleached, whitish ones. Some Indian grocers sell the seeds separately, a great convenience when grinding spice combinations such as *garam masala*. Many of my recipes call for whole cardamom pods. They are used as a flavouring and are not meant to be eaten. If a recipe calls for a small amount of ground cardamom seeds, pulverize them in a mortar.

CARDAMOM (ELAICHI)

LARGE BLACK
CARDAMOM (*BARI
ELAICHI*)

They look like black beetles and have an earthier, deeper flavour than green cardamom. Use them only when the recipe calls for them. They can be ground whole, skin and all.

CHANA DAL

See *Dals*.

CHAPATI FLOUR

A very finely ground wholewheat flour found only at Indian grocers and used for making Indian breads. If unavailable, use suggested combinations of wholewheat or wheatmeal flour and plain flour/white flour.

CHICKPEA FLOUR

Flour made out of chickpeas. In Indian shops it is known as gram flour or *besan*. It is also available in Britain in health food shops and in the United States in specialty stores where it is known as *farine de pois chiches*. I store mine in the refrigerator to discourage bugs.

CHILLIES, FRESH
HOT GREEN (*HARI
MIRCH*)

The fresh chillies used in India are 2–4 in/ 5–10 cm long and quite slim. They are generally green but sometimes ripen to a red colour and may be used just as easily. Besides being rich in vitamins A and C, their skins give Indian food a very special flavour. If other varieties of chillies are substituted, adjustments should be made as they could be very mild in flavour, such as 'Italian hot peppers' or wildly hot, such as the Mexican *jalapeño*.

To store fresh chillies, do not wash them. Just wrap them in newspaper and put them in a plastic container or plastic bag. Any chillies that go bad should be thrown away as they affect the whole batch.

All chillies should be handled with care especially when cut or broken. Refrain from touching your eyes or your mouth and wash your hands as soon as possible after you finish with them.

If you want the flavour of the green chilli skin

and none of its heat, remove its white seeds before cooking.

These chillies are generally 1 ½–2 ½ in/ 3.5–6 cm long and quite slim. They too should be handled with care, just like the fresh hot green chillies. If you want the flavour of the chillies, without their heat, make a small opening in them and shake out and discard their seeds.

WHOLE DRIED HOT RED (*SABUT LAL MIRCH*)

Indian refer to ground dried red chillies as red chilli powder. This is not the 'chilli powder' used in America to make Mexican 'chilli'. American 'chilli powder' is a spice mixture which includes ground cumin seeds. Because of this confusion, I have been forced to write 'red chilli powder' (cayenne pepper)', even though I'm aware that cayenne is a particular red chilli. For the purposes of this book, Indian red chilli powder and cayenne pepper are interchangeable.

CHILLI POWDER, RED/ CAYENNE PEPPER (*PISI HUI LAL MIRCH*)

When buying coconuts, make sure that they have no mould on them and are not cracked. Shake them to make sure that they are heavy with liquid. The more liquid the better. To break a coconut, hold the coconut in one hand over the sink and hit around the centre with the claw end of a hammer or the blunt side of a heavy cleaver. The coconut should crack and break into two halves. (The coconut water may be saved. It is generally not used in cooking but is very refreshing to drink.) Taste a piece of the coconut to make sure it is sweet and not rancid. Prise off the coconut flesh from the hard shell with a knife. If it proves to be too obstinate, it helps to put the coconut halves, cut side up, directly over a low flame, turning them around now and then so they char slightly. The woody shell contracts and releases the kernel.

Now peel off the brown coconut skin with a

COCONUT, GRATED FRESH

potato peeler and break the flesh into 1-in/ 2.5-cm pieces (larger ones if you are grating manually). Wash off these coconut pieces and either grate them finely on a hand grater or else put them in an electric blender or food processor. Do not worry about turning them into pulp in these electric machines. What you will end up with will be very finely 'grated' coconut, perfect for all the Indian dishes that require it.

Grated coconut freezes beautifully and defrosts fast. I always grate large quantities whenever I have the time and store it in the freezer for future use. (In America, excellent frozen grated coconut is available in some Mexican and Asian grocery stores. It is frozen in flat rectangles and defrosts very fast. It may be used in all my recipes that call for grated fresh coconut and may also be used to make coconut milk.)

COCONUT MILK, FRESH

Fill a glass measuring jug up to the ¾ pint/ 2 cup/ 450 ml mark with grated coconut. Empty it into a blender or food processor. Add ½ pint/ 1 ¼ cups/ 300 ml very hot water. Blend for a few seconds. Line a sieve with a piece of muslin or cheesecloth and place it over a bowl. Empty the contents of the blender into the sieve. Gather the ends of cloth together and squeeze out all the liquid. This is Thick Coconut Milk if the recipe calls for both thin and thick coconut milk. You should get about 12 fl oz/ 1 ½ cups/ 350 ml. To make Thin Coconut Milk, repeat the process with the coconut dregs and fresh hot water once or twice until you have the amount you require. If the recipe calls simply for Coconut Milk then follow the instructions for Thick Coconut Milk.

TINNED

Excellent quality tinned coconut milk is sold by most grocers who stock East Asian, South Asian or Latin American foods. You may use this in all my recipes. Make sure to buy *un*sweetened coconut milk. When you open the tin, stir its contents first as the cream tends to rise to the top. If the recipe calls for Thin and Thick Coconut Milk, go about it this way: buy two tins, each roughly ½ pint/ 1 ¼ cups/ 300 ml in capacity. For the Thin Coconut Milk, open one tin and scoop off the cream which rises to the top. Set the cream aside. Pour the remaining liquid into a measuring jug to make the required quantity. For the Thick Coconut Milk, open the second tin and stir its contents. As you happen to have a little extra coconut cream handy, this may be added to the contents of the second tin to make it extra rich.

MADE FROM CREAMED COCONUT

Creamed coconut is available fairly easily in Great Britain and in some Indian shops in Europe and the United States. It, too, may be used to make coconut milk. Put 5 (level) tbs/75 ml in a bowl. Slowly add ¼ pint/ ⅔ cup/ 150 ml of hot water and mix well. You should get about 8 fl oz/ 1 cup/ 250 ml of coconut milk. This may be used in any recipe that calls for Coconut Milk or Thick Coconut Milk. Where Thin Coconut Milk is required, put 5 tbs/ 75 ml in a bowl and slowly add ½ pint/ 1 ¼ cups/ 300 ml of hot water. This should give you about 12 fl oz/ 1 ½ cups/ 350 ml of thin coconut milk.

CORIANDER, FRESH GREEN/CHINESE PARSLEY (*HARA DHANIA*)

One of India's favourite herbs, this is used both as a seasoning and a garnish. Just the top leafy section is used.

To store fresh green coriander, put it, unwashed, roots and all, into a container filled with water, almost as if you're putting flowers in a vase. The leafy section of the plant should not be in water. Pull a plastic bag over the coriander and the container and refrigerate the whole thing. It should last for weeks. Every other day, discard any yellowing leaves.

CORIANDER SEEDS, WHOLE AND GROUND (*DHANIA, SABUT* AND *PISA*)

These are the round, beige seeds of the coriander plant. You may buy them already ground or you can buy whole seeds, and grind them yourself in small quantities in an electric coffee grinder. I like to put my home-ground coriander seeds through a sieve but this is not essential.

Ground coriander seeds, if stored for long, begin to taste a bit like sawdust. It is best at this stage to discard them and start with a fresh batch.

CORIANDER AND CUMIN SEED MIXTURE, GROUND (*DHANA ZEERA POWDER*)

This combination of roasted and ground coriander and cumin seeds, in the proportion of 4 parts to 1 part, is used in Gujarat and Maharashtra.

To make it, put 4 tbs/ ⅓ cup/ 60 ml of whole coriander seeds and 1 tbs/15 ml of whole cumin seeds into a small cast-iron frying pan and place the pan over a medium flame. Stir the seeds and keep roasting them until they turn a few shades darker. Let the seeds cool somewhat. Put the seeds into the container of a coffee grinder or other spice grinder and grind as finely as possible. Store in an airtight container.

CUMIN SEEDS, WHOLE AND GROUND (*ZEERA, SABUT* AND *PISA*)

Whole seeds keep their flavour well and may be ground very easily in an electric coffee grinder when needed. You may also buy the seeds in their ground form.

ROASTED AND GROUND (*BHUNA HUA ZEERA*)

Put 4–5 tbs/ 60–75 ml of whole cumin seeds into a small cast-iron frying pan and place the pan over a medium flame. Stir the seeds and keep roasting them until they turn a few shades darker. Let the seeds cool somewhat. Put the seeds into the container of a coffee grinder or other spice grinder and grind as finely as possible. Store in an airtight container.

BLACK (*SHAH ZEERA, SIYAH ZEERA* OR *KALA ZEERA*)

A caraway-like seed with a flavour that is more refined and complex than that of the ordinary cumin. As it is expensive, it is used in small quantities. If you cannot find it, use regular cumin seeds.

The highly aromatic curry leaves are shaped rather like bay leaves and are sold in India while still attached to their stems. Indian housewives and cooks use them only when they are fresh, pulling them off their stems just before they throw them into the pot. Only the dried leaves are available in most Western cities, though I notice that some grocers in Great Britain are now beginning to import them, fresh and on the stem, from Africa. There are sections of India, such as the South, where curry leaves flavour more than half the dishes. Use the fresh leaves whenever you can find them; otherwise resort to the less flavourful dried ones.

CURRY LEAVES, FRESH AND DRIED (*KARI PATTA*)

Technically, a *dal* is really a dried split pea though, even in India, the word is used rather loosely at times for all pulses (legumes), dried beans and split peas. Most split peas are sold in India in two forms, skinned and unskinned. It is the skinned variety, also known as 'washed', 'white' or '*dhuli dal*', that is used in this book.

DALS (DRIED SPLIT PEAS AND BEANS)

This is very much like the yellow split pea although it is smaller in size and sweeter in flavour. It is used as a spice in South India. Make sure you buy the skinned, split variety.

CHANA DAL

A hulled, salmon-coloured split pea, this is also known as red split lentil. If buying from an Indian shop, make sure you buy the skinned variety.

MASOOR DAL

Split *moong dal* or mung beans are sold both hulled and unhulled. My recipes call for only the skinned, all-yellow variety, also known as 'white' or 'washed'.

MOONG DAL

Also known as *toor dal* and *arhar dal*, this hulled, ochre-coloured split pea has quite a dark, earthy flavour. Make sure you buy the skinned variety,

TOOVAR DAL

sometimes called 'washed' or 'white'. Some shops sell an oily *toovar dal*. Here the *dal* has been rubbed with castor oil which acts as a preservative. The oil needs to be washed before the *dal* can be used. None of my recipes call for the oily *dal* though you may use it if the plain kind is not available.

URAD DAL

For this book, only buy the 'washed' or 'white' dal, ie, the skinned variety. This rather pale *dal* is used in the South for all kinds of savoury cakes and pancakes.

FENNEL SEEDS (SONF)

These seeds look and taste like anise seeds, only they are larger and plumper. They may be roasted (see the method for roasting cumin seeds) and used after meals as a mouth freshener and digestive. To grind fennel seeds, just put 2–3 tbs/ 45 ml into the container of a clean coffee grinder or other spice grinder and grind as finely as possible. Store in an airtight container.

FENUGREEK SEEDS (METHI)

Yellow, square and flattish, these seeds are meant to soothe the intestinal tract. They have a slightly bitter flavour and should not be allowed to burn.

FISH TAMARIND (KODAM POLI)

This sour rind of a special fruit – garcinia indica – is dried over wood smoke to make a black, sour, smoky seasoning that is particularly good with fish. It is used frequently in the cooking of Kerala. Before it is used, it should be rinsed off, sliced, and then given a quick soak for a few minutes to soften it a bit. If you cannot find it, use *kokum*, an unsmoked version of a fairly similar seasoning that is used further up the same West coast. It, too, needs to be rinsed off, sliced and soaked briefly. If you cannot find either *kodampoli* or *kokum*, lemon juice may be used as suggested in the specific recipes.

There are hundreds of spice mixtures in India, each used for different dishes in different ways. *Garam masala* is a highly aromatic mixture that is often sprinkled over the top of dishes that have almost finished cooking. There are many recipes for it. Here is mine. Take 1 tbs/ 15 ml cardamom seeds, 1 tsp/ 5 ml each whole black cumin seeds, whole cloves and black peppercorns, as well as about ⅓ of a nutmeg and a 2-in/ 5-cm cinnamon stick. Put them all into the container of a clean coffee grinder or other spice grinder and grind as finely as possible. Store in an airtight container.

GARAM MASALA

Put 3 × 1-in/ 2.5-cm cinnamon sticks, 15–20 whole cardamom pods and 8 whole cloves into the container of a clean coffee grinder or other spice grinder and grind as finely as possible. Store in an airtight container.

TO MAKE BENGALI
GARAM MASALA

This is butter that has been so well clarified that you can deep fry in it. Because it is totally free of all milk solids, it does not need refrigeration. *Ghee* has a very special, nutty taste. If you have access to Indian shops, my own advice would be that you buy ready-made *ghee*. The Netherlands, for example, exports an excellent quality which many Indian shops buy in bulk and then package in their own bottles. If you cannot buy ready-made *ghee*, here is how you go about making your own: take 1 lb/ 2 cups/ 450 g of the best quality unsalted butter that you can find. Put it in a heavy, smallish pan and let it melt over a low flame. Soon it will begin to simmer. Let it simmer on a low heat for about 45 minutes (timing really depends upon the amount of water in the butter), or until the milky solids turn brownish and either cling to the sides of the pan or else fall to the bottom. Because you have to boil all the water away without letting the butter brown, you must watch it, especially toward the end of the cooking time. Now strain the

GHEE

ghee through a quadrupled layer of cheesecloth. Homemade *ghee* is best stored covered in the refrigerator.

GINGER, DRIED, GROUND (*SONT*)

This is the ginger that is dried and ground (powdered), the same that you might use to make gingerbread. It is available in supermarkets.

GINGER, FRESH (*ADRAK*)

Known sometimes as ginger 'root', this is really a rhizome with a refreshing pungent flavour. Its potato-like skin needs to be peeled before it can be chopped or grated. To grate ginger, use the finest part of a hand grater. You should end up with a paste.

When buying ginger, look for pieces that are not too wrinkled and have a taut fresh skin. If you use ginger infrequently, you can 'store' it by planting it in somewhat dry sandy soil. Water infrequently. Your ginger will not only survive but may sprout fresh knobs. If you use ginger frequently, store in a cool airy basket along with your onions and garlic.

KARHAI

This is the Indian wok and may be made out of cast-iron or stainless steel. It is excellent for stir frying and its rounded bottom makes it very economical for deep frying.

KODAMPOLI

See Fish Tamarind.

MANGO

Many shops sell 'ripe' mangoes that are actually unripe and quite hard. You may ripen them yourself at home by wrapping them individually in newspaper and then storing them either in hay or in a basket. When they are ripe they should be very slightly soft to the touch and should begin to smell like mangoes. There should however, be no black spots on them. Once they are ripe they can be refrigerated.

MASOOR DAL

See *Dals*.

See *Dals*.

MOONG DAL

This yellow oil, made from mustard seeds, is quite pungent when raw, and sweet when heated to a slight haze. It is used all over India for pickling. In Kashmir and Bengal it is also used for everyday cooking and gives the foods of those regions their very special character. If you cannot find it, any other vegetable oil may be substituted. You might consider the rather unorthodox use of virgin olive oil. It has as much character and 'kick' as mustard oil, though of course the taste is completely different.

MUSTARD OIL (SARSON KA TEL)

These tiny dark round seeds, sometimes quite black, sometimes reddish-brown, are used throughout India for pickling and for seasoning everything from yoghurt to beans. They have a dual character. When popped in hot oil, they impart an earthy sweetness. However, when they are ground, they turn nose-tinglingly pungent and slightly bitter. Indians have developed a taste for this bitterness and consider it to be very good for their digestive systems. If you wish to cut down on the bitterness, use only freshly-bought black mustard seeds or use yellow mustard seeds.

MUSTARD SEEDS, WHOLE BLACK

These are commonly available and may be substituted for black mustard seeds should the latter prove elusive. They are less bitter and milder in flavour.

WHOLE YELLOW

See *Sambar* Powder.

MYSORE SAMBAR POWDER

These seeds are sometimes known, inaccurately, as onion seeds. They are little tear-shaped black seeds used throughout all of India for pickling. Some North Indian oven breads are dotted with them and in Bengal they are used commonly for cooking vegetables and fish.

NIGELLA SEEDS (KALONJI)

PANCHPHORAN (5-SPICE MIXTURE)

This very Bengali spice combination contains whole cumin seeds, whole fennel seeds, whole nigella seeds (*kalonji*), whole fenugreek seeds, and a tiny aromatic seed known in Bengal as *radhuni*. As *radhuni* is generally unavailable outside Bengal, even Indians, in India, use black mustard seeds as a substitute. You may buy ready-mixed *panchphoran* or you can put it together yourself by mixing 2 tsp/ 10 ml of whole cumin seeds, 2 tsp/ 10 ml of whole black mustard seeds. 2 tsp/ 10 ml of whole fennel seeds, 1 tsp/ 5 ml of nigella seeds (*kalonji*) and ¾ tsp/ 4 ml of whole fenugreek seeds. Store in an airtight container.

PAPADUM

Also called *papar*. These Indian wafers are generally made out of split peas and flavoured with red pepper, black pepper or garlic. *Papadums* made with sago flour or potato flour are also very popular in India. Keep what you do not use in a tightly sealed tin.

POPPY SEEDS, WHITE (*KHAS KHAS*)

These tiny white seeds can become rancid so they should be kept in a tightly closed bottle and stored in a cool place. You may even freeze poppy seeds. Blue poppy seeds are never used in India.

PRAWNS/SHRIMPS, HOW TO PEEL AND DEVEIN

Pull off the dangling legs as well as the head if it is there. Next, peel the shell from the body. Pull off the tail separately. To devein, make a shallow incision along the length of the prawn, right where the backbone would be if the prawn had one – all the way from head to tail. Here you will see a thread-like vein, often filled with black or green or yellow substance. Pull this out. If you do not find it, so much the better. Place all the peeled and deveined prawns in a bowl and wash them quickly under cold running water. Pat dry.

PULSES/LEGUMES

See *Dals*.

Also called rice powder, it has the same texture as corn flour and is sold in Indian and Oriental grocery stores.

RICE FLOUR

I have used only 'leaf' saffron here – the whole dried saffron threads. Find a good, reliable source for your saffron, as there is a great deal of adulteration.

SAFFRON

A South Indian spice mixture (p. 103).

SAMBAR POWDER, MYSORE

I use the beige, unhulled seeds. They have a wonderful nutty flavour especially after being roasted.

SESAME SEEDS (TIL)

This is the bean-like fruit of a tall tree. When ripe, it is peeled, seeded and compressed into brick-like shapes.

TAMARIND (IMLI)

To make tamarind paste: break off ½ lb/ 225 g from a brick of tamarind and tear into small pieces. Put in a stainless steel or a non-metallic bowl covered with ¾ pint/ 2 cups/ 450 ml of very hot water, and set aside for at least 3 hours or overnight. (In an extreme case when you need to use it instantly, you may simmer the tamarind for 10 minutes.) Set a sieve over a stainless steel or non-metallic bowl. Empty the soaked tamarind and its liquid into the sieve and push as much pulp through with your fingers or with the back of a wooden spoon as you can. Put whatever tamarind remains in the sieve back into the soaking bowl. Add 4 fl oz/ ½ cup/ 125 ml of hot water to it and mash it a bit. Return it to the sieve and try to extract some more pulp. Do not forget to collect all the thick, strained paste clinging to the bottom of your sieve. This quantity will make about 12 fl oz/ 1 ½ cups/ 350 ml. (Whatever tamarind remains in your sieve may be used for polishing brass!) Tamarind paste freezes well and will also last a good 2–3 weeks in the refrigerator. As long as it has no mould on it, you may use it.

TAVA

A slightly curved cast-iron griddle used in India for making breads. A cast-iron frying pan may be substituted.

TOOVAR DAL

See *Dals*.

TURMERIC

A rhizome of the ginger family with bright yellow flesh. Generally, only ground turmeric is available. It is made by boiling, drying and grinding the rhizome. In India it is considered an antiseptic.

URAD DAL

See *Dals*.

WHITE RADISH (MOOLI)

Long white radishes are sold in India with their leaves and the combination of vegetable and leaf is often cooked together. If you cannot find *mooli* with its leaves, substitute round or oval red radishes and their leaves.

INDEX TO THE RECIPES